WELCOME

Doesn't the beautiful game generate some magnificent stories? It seems the higher you go in football, the more intense the drama becomes. Take the Champions League for instance: from rank outsiders Marseille winning the inaugural trophy to Chelsea stalwart Didier Drogba sealing the 20th title, we have been witness to spectacle simply not present in other tournaments. We hope this MagBook represents a fitting tribute to what has become the most important club competition in the world.

Inside, we rank the tournament's 50 most successful clubs (pg10) – those who've reached the quarter-final stage and above – from Barcelona to Club Brugge via Monaco and Galatasaray: it's quite a trip. We also look back at every season: the stories, the scandals (there are plenty!) and the sensations. We pay homage to 20 Champions League Legends (pg72) – from Ronaldo to Zidane – and compile various top 10s from Memorable Moments (pg104) to Follicular Fails (pg116). We have also put together an A-Z covering everything from Roman Abramovich (pg4) to Zadok the Priest (pg9).

In short, if you're after a bitesize guide to the first 20 years of the Champions League or just want to whet your appetite for 2012/13, you're in the right place.

Stuart Messham, Editor

CONTENTS

THE A-Z
of the Champions League

From record viewing figures to possibly the best goal scored in a final, Europe's premier club competition has had an incredible two decades

is for

Abramovich, Roman

The world's 68th richest person (according to *Forbes*) and the owner of Chelsea FC, Roman Abramovich's interest in football was sparked while watching a Fernando Redondo-inspired Real Madrid beat Manchester United 2-3 at Old Trafford in a Champions League encounter on 19 April 2000. His billions have since changed the footballing landscape forever.

And also... Audience

In 2009, the Champions League final overtook the Super Bowl to become the most-watched annual sporting event in the world, with an estimated 109 million viewers. In the 2011/12 season, UEFA estimated that almost 200 million viewers tuned in across Australia, China, Japan, Korea and the Middle East for the group stages, and more than 300 million watched the final on TV. According to UEFA, 4.8 million tweets were sent concerning the final, the teams and the players, and, at the time of writing, the UEFA Champions League Facebook page had more than 2.75m 'likes'.

B is for

Barcelona

Winners of the Champions League three times, they were unlucky not to reach the 2011/12 final after defeat by an ultra-resilient Chelsea. They will, however, still be the team to beat in 2012/13, despite the rise of Paris St-Germain and Manchester City, the return to dominance of Juventus and losing La Liga to Real Madrid.

C is for

Comebacks

In the 1994/95 season, defending champions Milan began the group phase with a 2-0 defeat by Ajax and were deducted two points for crowd trouble against Casino Salzburg after their second matchday win. But despite having no points after two games, they still advanced from Group D and progressed all the way to the final, where they lost to Ajax and a single goal from Patrick Kluivert. Talking of comebacks, there is the small matter of a match in 1999 (pg 65) and a certain encounter in Istanbul (see 'I') to also consider...

D is for

Del Piero zone, the

Dutch hero Johan Cruyff has a change of motion named after him and Czechoslovakia's Antonin Panenka a cheeky penalty technique. But, as far as we know, no one had an area of the pitch named after them until Juventus's record appearance holder Alessandro Del Piero (above), began to score from the same spot, game after game. He would drop a shoulder, cut inside from the left, reach the Del Piero zone and then let fly with his right boot to score in the far top corner of the net (*Gol alla Del Piero*).

E is for

Experience

The oldest player to have featured in the Champions League is Lazio keeper Marco Ballotta (above), who was 43 years 252 days old when he faced Real Madrid in December 2007. Meanwhile, Roberto Di Matteo stuck with Chelsea's old guard, whom his predecessor, André Villas-Boas, had been freezing out, and helped the Blues to win the 2012 title. They may not have been another 'e' – entertaining – but experience told.

F is for

Ferguson, Sir Alex

The most successful Champions League manager, having won it twice and been runner-up twice. Famous for his penchant for 'hairdryers' and expensive red wine.

And also... Five!

In 2005, Liverpool were allowed to defend their Champions League title after being given special dispensation by UEFA. The Reds hadn't finished in the top four of the English Premier League (EPL) and were, therefore, not eligible to compete according to the governing body's criteria. But the ensuing public outcry persuaded UEFA to amend their qualification rulings: the top four sides *and* Liverpool were granted entry to the competition. It is the only time in Champions League history that five clubs from one country have qualified for the tournament. In 2011/12, Chelsea won the trophy and, despite finishing sixth in the EPL, will be allowed to defend their title this season – but this is at the expense of Tottenham Hotspur, who finished fourth in the league.

G is for

Goalscorers

You don't win the Champions League without having someone who gets his kicks from regularly hitting the back of the net. The quickest Champions League goal to date was scored by Roy Makaay (right) after 10 seconds, for Bayern Munich against Real Madrid on 7 March 2007. The fastest goal in a final was scored by Milan's Paolo Maldini, against Liverpool, after 52 seconds of the 2005 showpiece in Istanbul.

Lionel Messi is the undisputed king of Champions League net-busting though. He has been top scorer in the past four seasons and has the joint record for most goals in a Champions League season – 14 in 2011/12 (José Altafini scored the same amount for Milan in 1962/63). He is also the only player to have scored two hat-tricks in a Champions League season (against Viktoria Plzen and Bayer Leverkusen, again in 2011/12) and the only one to have scored five goals in one match in the Champions League era, during Barcelona's 7-1 destruction of Bayer Leverkusen in 2011/12.

And also... Group stages

The format of the European Cup changed in 1991, when a group phase was introduced, creating more games between Europe's biggest clubs. One group stage became two between 1999 and 2003 – by which time the competition was called the Champions League – but, since 2003, the now familiar one group phase followed by 16-team knockout has been in operation.

H is for

Hanot, Gabriel

Born on 6 November 1889, Gabriel Hanot was a French international footballer (he captained his country in 1919) who became a journalist after an aviation accident cut short his playing career. He became editor of *L'Equipe* (see 'L') and, alongside his colleague Jacques Ferran, was the principal visionary behind the European Cup.

It wasn't a scheme initially backed by UEFA: the two men simply approached the 16 clubs that they felt had the most fan appeal with a blueprint for the tournament and their rules were unanimously agreed upon. They then presented the plans to UEFA. On 4 September 1955, the first European Champions Clubs' Cup fixture was played in Lisbon, Sporting Clube de Portugal drawing 3-3 with FK Partizan. Hanot also initiated the Ballon d'Or award for European player of the season.

And also... Hat-tricks

The first hat-trick of the Champions League era was scored by PSV Eindhoven's Juul Ellerman against FK Zalgiris on 16 September 1992. Barcelona's Lionel Messi (below) is the only player to have scored two in one Champions League season, 2011/12 (see 'G'), which also featured the fastest hat-trick, scored by Olympique Lyonnais's Bafétimbi Gomis in seven minutes, during his side's 7-1 win over Dinamo Zagreb.

 (Messi, below right)

I is for

Istanbul

Perhaps the greatest ever comeback in a final. Three goals down to Milan at the break and looking decidedly buried, Liverpool didn't strive to avoid further embarrassment in the second half – they went on the attack and scored three of their own through Steven Gerrard (above), Vladimir Smicer and Xabi Alonso. Goalkeeper Jerzy Dudek's antics in the penalty shootout were enough to break the concentration of Milan's Andriy Shevchenko, who missed his kick to give Liverpool the Champions League trophy (see page 86).

J is for

Juventus

The Champions League's biggest losers (sort of), Juventus have lost the most finals – 3-1 to Borussia Dortmund in 1997; 1-0 to Real Madrid in 1998; and 3-2 on penalties to Milan in 2003. They've won one too though, 4-2 on penalties against Ajax in 1996.

K is for

Knockout

The European Cup used to be a straight knockout tournament featuring just the champions of each European league, playing home and away legs for each match. In 2010/11, teams that reached the knockout stage of the Champions League earned €3m. In its current format, the tournament has four knockout rounds after the group stage.

L is for

L'Equipe

Popular French daily sports paper that has had a great influence on the creation of the Tour de France and the European Cup. Gabriel Hanot (see 'H') first called for a European inter-club football competition in his column in December 1954.

M is for

Manchester United

The English Premier League's dominating force have qualified for Europe's premier competition 17 seasons in a row, a Champions League record. The last time they didn't qualify was in 1994/95, when Blackburn Rovers won the league.

And also... Money

The big money associated with Champions League football has altered the focus of clubs in every participant domestic league. Chelsea earned around £42m for lifting the trophy in May. Liverpool took £100,000 as Carling Cup winners.

N is for

New money

Recognising football's potential in expanding markets, mega-rich, far- and middle-eastern syndicates have acquired western clubs. Notably, Sheikh Mansour bought Manchester City – who won their first English Premier League title in 2011/12 – and the Qatar Investment Authority acquired Paris St-Germain. Neither club makes the current all-time Champions League table, but both will want to figure prominently on Europe's biggest stage next season.

O is for

One-club wonders

Only 19 players have made 100 or more Champions League appearances, and only 10 of these have made them for a single club: Paolo Maldini (Milan), Oliver Kahn (Bayern Munich), Ryan Giggs (Manchester United), Paul Scholes (Manchester United), Gary Neville (Manchester United), Iker Casillas (Real Madrid), Xavi (Barcelona), Carles Puyol (Barcelona, above), Roar Strand (Rosenborg BK) and Javier Zanetti (FC Internazionale).

P is for

Penalties

Whether you think penalties are a fair way to settle a clash between footballing behemoths, there's no doubt a shootout invokes drama unlike any other. Ten European finals have been decided by a shootout – Liverpool are the only team to have won more than one (1984 and 2005), while Juventus, Milan, Bayern Munich and Chelsea have won one and lost one. No team has lost a shootout twice.

And also... Platini, Michel

UEFA president since 2007, Michel Platini was not always a besuited executive bore, he was European Footballer of the Year in 1983, 1984 and 1985. At a time when European players were considered more robust and athletic than their South American counterparts, Platini stood out as a man who could caress and cajole a football

with the flavours of Rio and Buenos Aires, conducting play with the inside and outside of both feet. His UEFA incumbency has had its minor successes (see 'Q') but it will be his implementation of the European-wide Financial Fair Play Regulations that will be key going forward: trying to level the playing field now is certainly an unenviable task.

Q is for

Qualifying round

Since Michel Platini has been in the UEFA hotseat, the qualifying rounds have broadened somewhat, allowing some smaller nations in the UEFA co-efficient a better chance of appearing in the lucrative group stages. In 2008/09 a record four new teams managed it: Denmark's Aalborg, Romania's CFR Cluj, Cyprus's Anorthosis and Belarus's Bate Borisov.

R is for

Real Madrid

The most successful club in European Cup history, though not Champions League history, Real Madrid have won the tournament nine times – five times from 1955 to 1960, again in 1965/66 and three times in the Champions League era, 1997/98, 1999/00 and 2001/02.

S is for

Seedorf, Clarence

The Dutchman is the only player to win the Champions League four times with three clubs: Ajax in 1995, Real Madrid in 1998 and Milan in 2003 and 2007.

T is for

Top scorers

Rank	Player	Goals	Games	Goal ratio	Clubs
1	Raúl	71	144	0.49	Real Madrid, Schalke 04
2	Ruud van Nistelrooy	56	81	0.69	PSV, Manchester United, Real Madrid
3	Lionel Messi	51	68	0.75	Barcelona
4	Thierry Henry	50	114	0.44	Monaco, Arsenal, Barcelona
5	Andriy Shevchenko	48	102	0.47	Dynamo Kyiv, Milan, Chelsea
6	Filippo Inzaghi	46	83	0.55	Parma, Juventus, Milan
7	Alessandro Del Piero	42	96	0.43	Juventus
8	Didier Drogba	39	75	0.52	Marseille, Chelsea
	Cristiano Ronaldo	39	83	0.47	Manchester United, Real Madrid
10	Fernando Morientes	33	93	0.35	Real Madrid, Monaco, Liverpool, Valencia, Marseille

U is for

UEFA

The Union of European Football Associations was founded in 1954, comprises 53 members and – like the other continental associations CONCACAF, CONMEBOL, CAF, AFC and OFC – works under the supervision of the global governing body, FIFA. UEFA runs international and club competitions, controlling the rights and prize money associated with them. Henri Delaunay, the Frenchman behind the European Championship, was its first general secretary.

And also... Underdogs

Despite accusations that the Champions League was making the people's game more about money than joy – resulting in the rise of the *Galácticos* regime and super-rich benefactors – football does still have the ability to surprise. Under José Mourinho in 2004, Porto lifted the trophy (right) with 10 Portuguese starters in the final against AS Monaco, beating Manchester United, Lyon and Deportivo La Coruna en

route. Also, in 2004/05, an unfancied Liverpool side became the first team in the history of the competition to reach the knockout phase from the first qualifying round.

V is for

Vieira, Patrick

The Frenchman is the only player to have been sent off for three different teams in the Champions League – for Arsenal v PSV Eindhoven in 2004; for Juventus v Club Brugge in 2005, and for Internazionale v Sporting Lisbon in 2006.

And also... Vote, UEFA

In the autumn of 1991, UEFA assembled a 35-member congress that granted all television and commercial rights to a new continent-wide mini-league system. A year later it began and was named the Champions League.

W

Wembley

To mark the 150th anniversary of the Football Association in 2013, England's most famous stadium will host the UEFA Champions League final for an unprecedented second time in three years, having also hosted in 2010/11.

X is for

Xavi

Spain's foremost proponent of the short-passing, high-pressing tiki-taka style of play and the heartbeat of the hugely successful Barcelona team that has dominated the Champions League under Pep Guardiola. Frequently makes more passes in one match than the whole of the opposition's midfield.

Y is for

Youth

The youngest player to score a hat-trick in the Champions League is Wayne Rooney. Aged 18 years 335 days he bagged three goals on his Champions League and Manchester United debut against Fenerbahçe on 28 September 2004, in a 6–2 home win. The youngest goalscorer is Ghanaian Peter Ofori-Quaye, who scored for Olympiacos v Rosenborg on 1 October 1997, aged 17 years 195 days. Josh McEachran (1 March 1993, above) is the first player born after the Champions League started (25 November 1992) to take part in the competition. He was a substitute for Chelsea v Zilina in September 2010.

Z is for

Zadok the Priest

The Champions League anthem is an arrangement by Tony Britten of George Frideric Handel's *Zadok the Priest*. It was commissioned by UEFA in 1992 and its chorus contains the three official languages used by the governing body: English, German and French. It has never been commercially released but withing a few notes of it beginning everyone knows which association to make. A consummate piece of branding by UEFA.

And also... Zinedine Zidane

Widely regarded, along with Lionel Messi, as the greatest player to have graced the Champions League, Zinedine Zidane (right) finished as a runner-up with Juventus in 1996/97 and 1997/98. But he won the competition in his first season at Real Madrid in 2001/02, scoring arguably the best European Cup final goal with a technically brilliant, quite outrageous, left-footed volley. It's worth noting, he was predominantly right-footed.

THE
TEAMS

||||||||||||||||||||||||||||||||||||||||||||||||||||||||||||||||||||||||||

Full name **Futbol Club Barcelona** | Nickname **Barça** | Founded **1899** | Ground **Camp Nou** (Capacity 99,354)

BARCELONA

Purveyors of some of the finest football Europe has ever seen

CLUB FACTFILE

Club homepage
fcbarcelona.com

Rivals Real Madrid

CL Seasons 17

QF appearances 11

SF appearances 9

Final appearances 3

CHAMPIONS LEAGUE ★STAR

Lionel Messi

Appearances 214

2004 - Present

Despite all of his individual awards (he won the Ballon d'Or for three seasons in a row from 2009-11) Lionel Messi is an unselfish team player who extracts the best qualities from his team-mates. Whereas Cristiano Ronaldo – his main rival for the title of best player in the world – tends to have more selfish footballing attributes, Messi appears born to play Barcelona's short-passing, tiki-taka style. Alongside Xavi and Andrés Iniesta, the diminutive Argentinian has made it the most coveted playing style in world football.

LIQUID FOOTBALL

Few results in Champions League history have turned quite so many heads as Barcelona's shock exit from the 2012 tournament at the hands of eventual winners Chelsea. In the semi-final, with their noses in front and facing an opposition reduced to 10 men, Barcelona uncharacteristically conceded and then failed to break down their opponents at the Nou Camp.

It signalled the end of an extraordinary era for the club. Not long afterwards, their coach of the past four years, Pep Guardiola, announced he was leaving.

To say Guardiola had been an inspired appointment for Barcelona would be putting it mildly. His team played some of the finest football ever seen in European competition – a breathtaking attacking style that had brought them Champions League success in 2009 and 2011 (the last two of Barça's four triumphs).

DID YOU KNOW?
Barcelona have played in one European competition or another every season since 1955

DOMESTIC DOMINANCE

On the home front, too, Barcelona's approach has reaped dividends. Three La Liga titles on the trot before Real Madrid took the crown last season – but even that disappointment was offset by victory in the Copa del Rey. The club recorded a rare treble in 2009, winning Spain's two main prizes, on top of their Champions League triumph. In all, Barcelona have won 21 Spanish league titles.

WHERE NEXT?

FC Barcelona stands at a crossroads. Guardiola's assistant, Tito Vilanova, has moved into the hot seat, still working with players of the calibre of Lionel Messi, David Villa and Cesc Fábregas, and he's schooled in the mentality of his predecessor. But while Barcelona are strong contenders to reclaim their domestic title and the Champions League trophy, there's a suspicion their dominance may be fading.

Still, as one of the finest teams to watch ever, Barça have no shortage of people who salute their success and how they have achieved it. Whether that success continues, or the club returns to the relative drought of the 1970s, remains to be seen.

Full name **Manchester United Football Club** | Nickname **The Red Devils** | Founded **1878** | Ground **Old Trafford** (75,811)

MAN UTD

One of the giants of English football, and a modern-day European force too

CLUB FACTFILE

Club homepage
manutd.com

Rivals Manchester City

CL Seasons 18

QF appearances 12

SF appearances 7

Final appearances 4

CHAMPIONS LEAGUE ★STAR

Ryan Giggs

Appearances 909

1987 - Present

A Manchester United stalwart and the most decorated player in English football history, Ryan Giggs – with his experience, skill and versatility – has morphed from an electric winger to a cogitative midfielder. Still tireless and passionate at 38 years of age, Giggs was recently handed the captaincy of Team GB at the London Olympics and brought out the best in his young charges. If the Welshman can push on to make his 1,000th appearance for Manchester United, it will be a benchmark celebrated across the football world.

GOLDEN ERA

Manchester United were two minutes from clinching a 20th English league title at the end of the 2011/12 season, but a late intervention from their fierce rivals Manchester City turned things around. It meant United finished without a trophy in what was a difficult season for the club, as Sir Alex Ferguson presses on with building yet another title-challenging team.

Under Ferguson's stewardship, the Red Devils have been reunited with their former glories, with 21 domestic league and cup successes. Given the rich heritage of the club, it's no small achievement that Ferguson's tenure has been their most fruitful.

THE COMPETITION

But there are signs that United's dominance may not be quite what it was. Chelsea have seized several titles from under United's nose, while City's chequebook has added another strong competitor to the field. Meanwhile, in 2011/12, United failed to get past the group stages of the Champions League for only the second time since the mid-1990s, and they fared equally poorly in the Europa League, crashing out to Athletic Bilbao. However, write them off at your peril.

United have won two Champions League titles in the past 15 years, including a dramatic last-minute turnaround against Bayern Munich in 1999. They were also beaten finalists as recently as 2011 and, as Ferguson rebuilds his team, they will undoubtedly be a force to be reckoned with on future European stages.

DID YOU KNOW?
Manchester United were the first English team to lift the European Cup, under Matt Busby in 1968

Before Ferguson led them to the Cup Winners' Cup in 1991, to bring European glory back to Old Trafford, the club's only other victory on the continent had been their 1968 European Cup victory.

LOOKING AHEAD

United's future in Europe doesn't look easy, but it might still be bright. Since they were comprehensively outplayed by Barcelona in the 2011 Champions League final, the team have gone through a period of transition and a new generation will take the club forward. Ferguson, at least for the next year or two, will be there to guide them.

|||||||||||||||||||||||||||||||||||||||||||||||||||||||||||||||||||||||||||||||||||||||||||||||||||||||

Full name **Associazione Calcio Milan** | Nickname **i Rossoneri (The Red and Blacks)** | Founded **1889** | Ground **Giuseppe Meazza** (80,018)

AC MILAN

Huge in the 1980s and 90s, AC Milan are proving they are no slouches today, either

CLUB FACTFILE

Club homepage
acmilan.com

Rivals Inter Milan

CL Seasons 15

QF appearances 9

SF appearances 7

Final appearances 6

CHAMPIONS LEAGUE ★STAR

Filippo Inzaghi

Appearances 202

2001-2012

A veritable 'fox in the box', Filippo Inzaghi may not have been tremendously exciting to behold – after all, he didn't have the pure skill of Ronaldo, the impudence of Zlatan Ibrahimovich or the sheer class of Andriy Shevchenko – but he was second-to-none at being in the right place at the right time. At the peak of his powers, Inzaghi was the greatest goal-poacher on the continent and exactly the kind of player you could rely on to make the difference on the very big occasions. Never hid, always made his mark.

LATIN MASTERS

AC Milan have been crowned champions of Europe seven times, a record second only to that of Real Madrid. In addition, they have won two Cup Winners' Cups and five UEFA Super Cups – a European honours list no other Italian team can match.

Milan's best era kicked off in the mid-1980s, when they had an influx of star names such as Ruud Gullit, Marco van Basten and Frank Rijkaard. The three Dutch players were part of a team that was named as the best club side of all time – and little wonder. They brought more than 20 trophies to the club, including three European Cups in five years. Perhaps none are quite as memorable as their 4-0 demolition of Barcelona in 1994, a scoreline that, now, would be unthinkable.

STEADY AS YOU GO

Between 1988 and 1995, Milan were also twice losing finalists in Europe's premier club competition, including being on the wrong end of a 1-0 scoreline against Marseille in the first Champions League final in May 1993. Unlike some of their contemporaries, though, Milan haven't gone through a dramatic fall in the past decade or two, nor have they been hit by huge financial problems. The closest they came was when they were caught up in the Italian match-fixing scandal of 2006. They were deducted 15 points (reduced to eight on appeal), which meant the club still qualified for the 2006/07 Champions League. Almost inevitably, they won it – 2-1 against Liverpool thanks to Filippo Inzaghi's two goals – the last time they have done so.

DID YOU KNOW?
AC Milan is owned by ex-prime minister of Italy Silvio Berlusconi, whose funds aided their mid-1980s turnaround

ITALIAN RENAISSANCE?

In recent years, Italian teams haven't fared as well in the Champions League as they historically have done – and AC Milan are no exception. Their quarter-final appearance in 2011/12 – when they were beaten by Barcelona, 3-1 on aggregate – was their best performance in the competition since their 2007 triumph.

Still, Milan were snapping at the heels of Juventus for the Serie A title last season and they continue to demonstrate real strength. An outside bet for triumph in 2013, then.

Full name **Real Madrid Club de Fútbol** | Nickname **Los Blancos (The Whites)** | Founded **1902** | Ground **Bernabéu** (85,454)

REAL MADRID

When it comes to money, Real Madrid have a lot of it

CLUB FACTFILE

Club homepage
realmadrid.com

Rivals Barcelona

CL Seasons 16

QF appearances 10

SF appearances 7

Final appearances 3

CHAMPIONS LEAGUE ★STAR

Zinedine Zidane

Appearances 155

2001-2006

Talked about in the same reverential tones as world footballing greats Diego Maradona and Johan Cruyff, when Algeria-born Zinedine Zidane stepped on to a pitch, he did the most difficult of things: make football look easy. Voted World Footballer of the Year in 1998, 2000 and 2003, Zidane could dribble, score regularly with both feet and his head, change the pace and the direction of a game with a single move, and generally upset the opposition with his vast array of genius. A true great.

HARD CASH

Welcome to one of the richest football clubs on Earth. Real Madrid's longstanding success has brought it a consistent revenue stream and a fan base that spans the globe. Furthermore, now the extreme *galactico* era of buying star player after star player has passed (although big-name signings are still to be found), there are indications that Real may be re-exerting their grip on the Spanish domestic scene.

Under current boss José Mourinho, they claimed a record 32nd La Liga title in 2012. It was their first league success since 2008 and was won at the expense of their fierce rivals, Barcelona. Real's football was less expansive, but Mourinho has formed a hard team to beat.

INTO EUROPE

It'll be interesting to see how well his team adapts to European competition. In the past two years, Real have reached the semi-finals of the Champions League, but for six years in a row they hadn't progressed past the last 16. Given that Real Madrid have won Europe's top prize nine times – more than any other team – that's slim pickings. Mourinho's reign will only really be regarded as a success if he brings them their tenth crown and the signs are he's edging closer to doing so, having recently signed a new contract with the club.

The last time Real Madrid won the Champions League was in 2002, when they beat Bayer Leverkusen 2-1 at Hampden Park. Otherwise most of their European glory came in the 1950s and 1960s, when they enjoyed six of their triumphs. They also added two UEFA Cup wins in the 1980s.

INTIMIDATING

Being one of only three teams never to have been relegated from La Liga, with a squad full of world-class footballing talent, Real Madrid show little sign of losing their position as one of the powerhouses of Spanish and European football anytime soon. Backed by some of the most passionate supporters in the world, who make the Bernabéu an intimidating place for away teams, their fate may still depend on how well Barcelona adapt to life without Pep Guardiola.

DID YOU KNOW?
Cristiano Ronaldo cost Real Madrid £80m – but 111 goals in 102 appearances is a good return on the investment

Full name **Fußball-Club Bayern München eV** | Nickname **Der FCB (The FCB)** | Founded **1900** | Ground **Allianz Arena** (69,901)

BAYERN MUNICH

Four-times European champions, but with a habit of also losing it late

CLUB FACTFILE

Club homepage
fcbayern.t-home.de

Rivals FC Nuremburg

CL Seasons 15

QF appearances 11

SF appearances 6

Final appearances 4

CHAMPIONS LEAGUE ★ STAR

Oliver Kahn

Appearances 429

1994-2008

Utterly dependable, unashamedly imposing and avidly Bavarian, Oliver Kahn guarded Der FCB's sticks for 14 years and brought great strength and honour to the biggest football club in Germany. He would come out from his goal to claim the ball at players' feet like a Bavarian steam train and commanded his area at set-pieces unlike any other goalkeeper before him. As such, Kahn was a centre-back's dream. Probably the most intimidating goalkeeper ever to stalk the six yard box, and a true legend for Bayern Munich.

ENGLISH CURSE

German giants Bayern Munich must hate playing English teams in the Champions League final. In 2011/12, they were minutes from a 1-0 win over Chelsea when Didier Drogba's late headed goal took the game to extra time and penalties, which Munich lost 4-3. Then, of course, there was 1999, when their name was virtually on the trophy before stoppage-time goals from Teddy Sheringham and Ole Gunnar Solskjaer gave Manchester United the victory, 2-1. Few finals have ended so dramatically.

That said, when Bayern Munich lifted the trophy in 1975 it was courtesy of a 2-0 win over Leeds United. Their most recent Champions League victory was in 2001, a 5-4 penalty shootout win over Valencia, and they lost the 2010 final 2-0 to Inter Milan – but they remain a side to be feared in Europe.

RICH HERITAGE

Bayern Munich's most successful period was arguably in the 1960s and 70s, but the club have won the Bundesliga title five times in the past decade, and were runners-up in the league in 2011/12 (although they finished eight points behind winners Borussia Dortmund). Munich have not been outside of the top three in the Bundesliga since 2007 and, during that time, have enjoyed success in two of the domestic cup competitions.

DID YOU KNOW?

Bayern Munich won the European Cup three times in a row in the 1970s – in 1974, 1975 and 1976

HIGH TURNOVER

It has not all been happy and wonderfully consistent behind the scenes at the Allianz Arena, however. Of late, Bayern Munich have burned through coaches and, as a result, have lacked the consistency that Ottmar Hitzfeld brought to them in his six-year spell from 1998, when he brought glory back to Munich. (Hitzfeld returned to the club in 2007 for a brief and less successful stint.)

The current manager, Jupp Heynckes, will be expected to close the gap on Dortmund in 2012/13, although – given that he was minutes from bringing Europe's top prize back to Munich – he should get another season to try to go one better. Ultimately, Bayern have a long heritage of success on the domestic and European stages.

Full name **Juventus Football Club** | Nickname **La Vecchia Signora (The Old Lady)** | Founded **1897** | Ground **Juventus Stadium** (41,000)

JUVENTUS

They have climbed back to the top of Italian football in style – now for Europe

CLUB FACTFILE

Club homepage juventus.com

Rivals Inter Milan

CL Seasons 12

QF appearances 7

SF appearances 5

Final appearances 4

CHAMPIONS LEAGUE ★ STAR

Alessandro Del Piero

Appearances 705

1993-2012

Juventus had so much faith in Alessandro Del Piero as a teenager, that they were happy to let Roberto Baggio – 'The Divine Ponytail' – transfer to rivals AC Milan. Their confidence proved well placed. Not the quickest, Del Piero would carve out his best work between the defensive lines, drawing in defenders, then passing or beating them out of the game. Nineteen years after he made his debut – a plethora of black-and-white success behind him – he would retire a club legend and king of the *trequartistas*.

SURVIVING A SCANDAL

It's fair to say Juventus are recovering from one of the toughest periods in their history. It's not just that they were relegated to Serie B for the first time in 2006 – it's the reason why. One of five clubs implicated in a match-rigging scandal, Juventus were stripped of the league titles they won in 2005 and 2006, were relegated, and forced to battle back to Serie A.

They did so by the start of the 2007/08 season and, in 2011/12 – under former Juventus player Antonio Conte – they completed their recovery with an extraordinary Serie A title-winning season. They went the entire campaign unbeaten, the first team to do so in the 38-game format of the league.

EUROPEAN DREAM

The next challenge for Juventus is to revive their reputation in continental competition. The club's trophy cabinet isn't short of European silverware – two European titles, the Cup Winners' Cup, a trio of UEFA Cups and assorted other victories. The most recent was their Champions League win of 1996, when they beat Ajax 4-2 on penalties. Juventus also reached the final in 1997 and 1998, but lost to Borussia Dortmund (3-1) and Real Madrid (1-0) respectively. Since then, they have suffered a drought in terms of European success, save for another final appearance in 2003, when they lost a drab match 3-2 on penalties to AC Milan at Old Trafford.

Other Italian teams, such as Milan and Inter, have somewhat usurped Juventus in Europe and they have not made it past the last 16 since their 2006 quarter-final appearance.

COME AGAIN

There's a sense, though, that the club are poised for another big push on Europe. They are over their well-documented problems and the manner in which they won Serie A in 2012 suggests a steely resolve. This will serve Juventus well in Europe and, combined with the natural defensive excellence of Italian teams playing on the continent, may make them a good outside bet for this year's trophy.

> **DID YOU KNOW?**
> Despite their troubles, Juventus are still Italy's most successful club, with 28 league titles and nine Italian cup wins

Full name **Chelsea Football Club** | Nickname **The Blues** | Founded **1905** | Ground **Stamford Bridge** (41,837)

CHELSEA

The reigning champions of Europe get set to defend their title

CLUB FACTFILE

Club homepage
chelseafc.com

Rivals Arsenal

CL Seasons 10

QF appearances 8

SF appearances 6

Final appearances 2

CHAMPIONS LEAGUE ★ STAR

Didier Drogba

Appearances 226

2004-2012

The most powerful striker the Premier League has seen, Didier Drogba combined, to great effect, his brute strength with the more subtle qualities needed by a modern striker: pace, power, the ability to assist and hold up the ball, and the ability to break beyond. Always contributed to the Blues' cause on the big occasions and was deservedly the main man during their victorious Champions League campaign of 2011/12. You could be sure that wherever Drogba went in the blue of Chelsea, drama would follow.

THE CHAMPIONS

Chelsea's Russian billionaire owner Roman Abramovich saw his European dream realised in 2012, when the Blues secured the Champions League trophy for the first time. It marked the end of a dramatic journey for the club.

Seemingly heading out of the competition under then-manager André Villas-Boas, temporary boss Roberto Di Matteo masterminded a memorable semi-final victory over Barcelona (despite his side being down to 10 men for most of the second leg after John Terry was sent off) and then a dramatic penalty shootout success over Bayern Munich in the final. No wonder Di Matteo was given the job permanently.

Chelsea had been a penalty shootout from winning the trophy before, of course, but Terry scuffed his kick in the 2008 final in Moscow and Manchester United prevailed. The 2012/13 season will be their tenth consecutive appearance in the tournament and they have qualified by virtue of last season's win rather than their Premier League finish (fifth).

> **DID YOU KNOW?**
> In his bid to win the Champions League, Abramovich has spent more than £1bn on player wages and transfers

HIRED AND FIRED

The Abramovich era has been defined by (mostly domestic) trophies, impatience and a managerial merry-go-round. Chelsea looked steadiest under José Mourinho and Carlo Ancelotti, but both fell foul of the Russian and were sacked.

In terms of honours, the past decade has brought three Premier League titles, four FA Cups, one League Cup and Champions League success. Had Abramovich had more patience – especially with the spiky Mourinho – it could have been more. That said, this is a golden era for Chelsea, who previously had one league title and a few domestic cups to their name.

FRESH FACES

The challenge now is to replace an ageing squad. Champions League hero Didier Drogba left in the close season, while Terry, Frank Lampard and Ashley Cole are all in their 30s. A lot is expected from new signing Eden Hazard, but Abramovich has deep pockets and these could be the difference between one-off Champions League success or the start of something bigger.

Full name **Liverpool Football Club** | Nickname **The Reds** | Founded **1897** | Ground **Anfield** (45,522)

LIVERPOOL

The team that won the most incredible Champions League final of all time

CLUB
FACTFILE

Club homepage
liverpoolfc.com

Rivals Man Utd

CL Seasons 8

QF appearances 5

SF appearances 3

Final appearances 2

CHAMPIONS LEAGUE
★ STAR

Steven Gerrard

Appearances 586

1998-Present

The English Premier League title has eluded Liverpool's talisman, but Steven Gerrard guided the Reds to triumph in the 2005 Champions League. En route, he showed all the football qualities that have installed him as a club legend. He was inspiring, driving, scored brilliant, vital goals, and, most importantly, he never gave up – a quality that has epitomised his career. Whether we'll see Gerrard in the Champions League again depends on whether new manager Brendan Rodgers can change around the Reds' ailing fortunes.

THRILLING ENDS

There are several candidates for the most extraordinary Champions League final to date. Manchester United's late, late show against Bayern Munich in 1999 was probably the leading contender – that is until Liverpool took on AC Milan on 25 May 2005.

Conceding a goal within the first minute and 3-0 down at the break, Liverpool were seemingly down and out in Istanbul. But their second-half comeback is the stuff of fairytales. Within 15 minutes of the restart they were level and the game went to a penalty shootout, which Liverpool won.

It was the fifth time the Reds had been crowned champions of Europe – the most of any English side – and it came at a point when the club's domestic dominance had long since become a thing of the past.

Liverpool were the premier side in England in the 1980s, but last lifted the league title in 1990, and the current team – under new manager Brendan Rodgers – still seem a long way from winning it back and restoring former glories to Anfield.

DID YOU KNOW?
Liverpool didn't qualify for the 2005/06 Champions League, but were allowed in to defend their title win

TROPHY ENVY

That said, Liverpool's history is littered with enviable success. It is only recently that their record of 18 English league titles has been surpassed by Manchester United and to that tally Liverpool have added seven FA Cups and eight League Cups (the last of these in 2011/12). Their success in Europe isn't restricted to the Champions League, either. The Reds' 2001 UEFA Cup triumph, for instance, was an amazing 5-4 victory over Alaves, with an own goal by Delfi Geli giving Liverpool a golden-goal triumph.

TOUGH TASK

The broader challenge for Liverpool is clear. Rodgers, brought in after the sacking of Kenny Dalglish, will be tasked with getting the club to challenge for top honours again. In the first instance, the minimum requirement will be qualification for the Champions League, in which the Reds will not feature in 2012/13 – the third season in a row that they have missed out. But surrounded by teams with more financial clout, Liverpool may be facing one of their toughest challenges.

Quite simply *the* greatest player in the world at the moment, Barcelona's Lionel Messi is the closest Europe has come to replicating the lyrical motions of Diego Maradona, a fellow Argentinian, during his spell at Napoli from 1984 to 1991.

UEFA

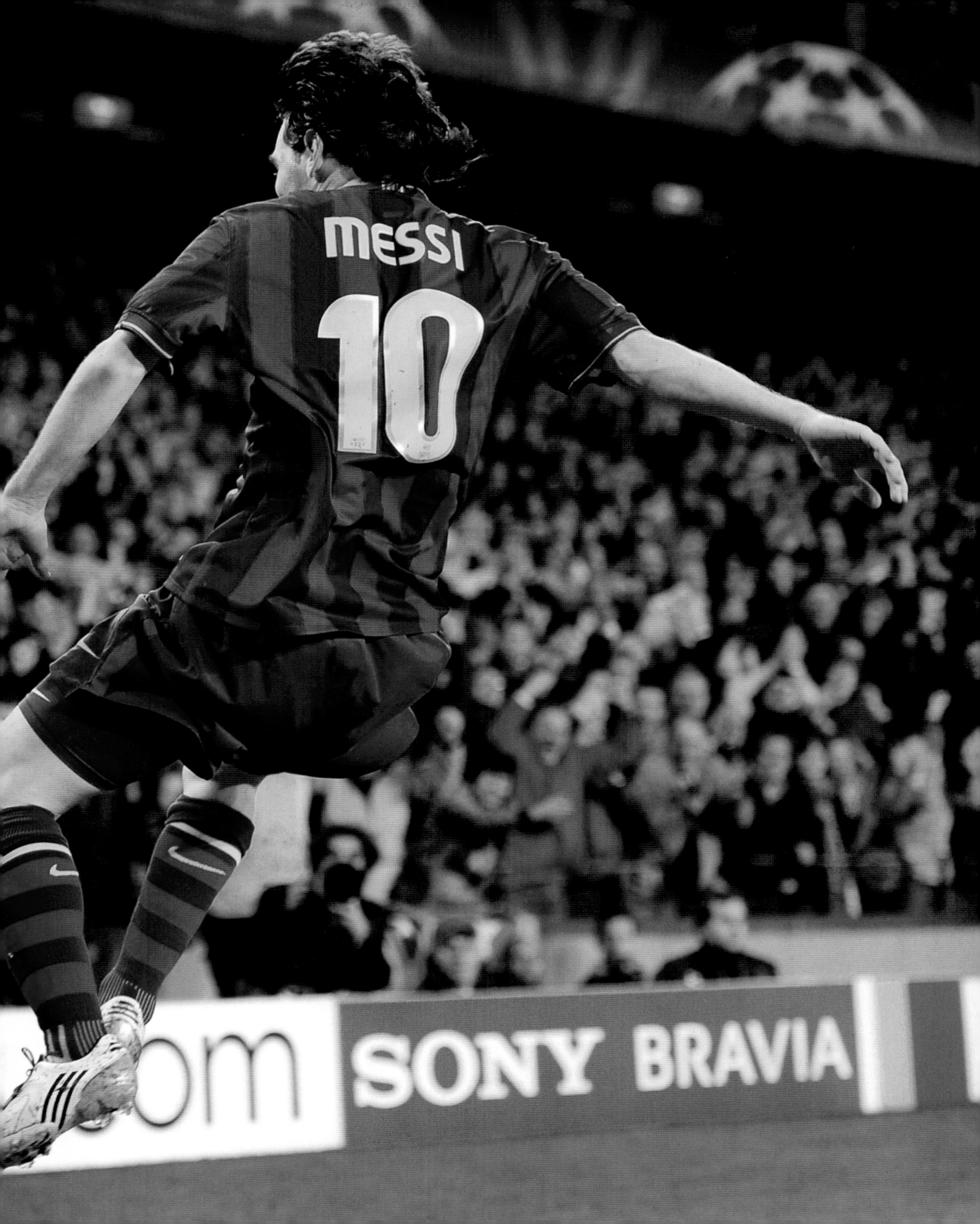
MESSI
10
SONY BRAVIA

|||||||||||||||||||||||||||||||||||||||||||||||||||||||||||||||||||||||||||||||||||||||||||||||||||||||

Full name **Amsterdamsche Football Club Ajax NV** | Nickname **De Godenzonen (Sons of gods)** | Founded **1900** | Ground **Amsterdam Arena** (53,342)

AJAX

Purveyors of Total Football who have lost their way in Europe

CLUB FACTFILE

Club homepage
ajax.nl

Rivals Feyenoord

CL Seasons 13

QF appearances 4

SF appearances 3

Final appearances 2

CHAMPIONS LEAGUE ★STAR

Frank Rijkaard

Appearances 261

1980-1987 and 1993-1995

Just 17 when he made his debut for Ajax in 1980, Frank Rijkaard returned to the club in 1993 and spent his last moments on a pitch with *De Godenzonen*, stirring his youthful team-mates to an unlikely Champions League victory over AC Milan in Vienna. At times he was faultless, whether he played in defence or slightly higher up the pitch, protecting his back four. A combination of great vision and execution usually marked him out as *the* best player in some very, very good teams. A one-off.

STYLE AND SUBSTANCE

In 2011/12, Ajax lifted the Eredivisie title for the 31st time, finishing six points ahead of Feyenoord and so retaining the trophy they'd won the season before, after an uncharacteristic gap of seven years.

The club have had several golden eras, but few are remembered as fondly as the late 1960s and early '70s, when the concept of Total Football was brought mesmerisingly to life. Until Barcelona picked up the mantle in recent years, no team enjoyed so much success in Europe playing such delicious football. Ajax proved you can win trophies *and* entertain on a level that had rarely been seen before.

END OF AN ERA

Their style of play resulted in three consecutive European Cup wins between 1971 and 1973, but by the middle of the decade star players such as Johan Cruyff had moved on and Ajax's glory days were fading. They didn't win again in Europe until 1987, when they secured the Cup Winners' Cup after a 1-0 win over Lokomotive Leipzig. Ajax were still picking up domestic trophies, adding several league titles every decade, as well as cup wins. They would conquer Europe again in 1995, when they beat holders and favourites Milan 1-0 in the Champions League final thanks to a goal from Patrick Kluivert, six minutes from time.

DID YOU KNOW?
Ajax are officially ranked as the seventh most successful European club of the 20th century

LEAN TIMES

The victory topped a season in which Ajax were also unbeaten in the league, but, sadly, it was a turning point for the club. Several key players moved on in the subsequent years and, while Ajax have continued to enjoy domestic success, their European fortunes have been less impressive.

They usually have enough about them to battle their way out of the Champions League group stage, but they usually fall soon afterwards and you have to go back to 2003 for the last time they made the quarter-finals of the competition.

At their peak, Ajax were one of the most exciting teams ever to grace the European stage – but a new golden era doesn't appear to be with us just yet.

Full name **Football Club Internazionale Milano** | Nickname **I Nerazzurri (The Black and Blues)** | Founded **1908** | Ground **San Siro** (80,018)

INTER MILAN

From riches, to near-relegation, to riches again

CLUB
FACTFILE

Club homepage
inter.it

Rivals AC Milan

CL Seasons 12

QF appearances 6

SF appearances 2

Final appearances 1

CHAMPIONS
LEAGUE
★STAR

Diego Milito

Appearances 91

2009-Present

At the age of 30, Argentina striker Diego Milito finally realised his potential as one of Europe's most dangerous marksmen under the guidance of José Mourinho in the 2009/10 season. He scored six times for Inter Milan in the Champions League to secure a well-deserved winner's medal and complete a league, cup and European treble in his first season with the club. After the departure from Inter of Mourinho, and because of a recurring knee injury, Milito has not enjoyed the same levels of success since.

HERITAGE

Success is expected at Inter Milan, a team who have been in the top flight of Italian football, without interruption, since 1929. In that time they have amassed 30 domestic trophies, including 18 Serie A titles, five of which were consecutive between 2006 and 2010, a joint-record in Italian football.

Inter Milan have managed to replicate some of that success in Europe, too. Their Champions League victory in 2010 was the third time they have been crowned kings of Europe (although it was their first success for 35 years, having won the European Cup two seasons in a row, in 1964 and 1965).

Diego Milito scored both goals as Inter Milan defeated Bayern Munich 2-0 in Madrid and, in doing so, completed a rare treble of winning the league, cup and Champions League in the same season.

COMING BACK

The treble-winning season marked something of a re-emergence for Inter, after one of the darkest eras in the club's history. At one stage, in 1994, they teetered on the verge of relegation to Serie B for the first time and only survived by a single point.

While they won the UEFA Cup three times in the 1990s, Inter Milan were regularly outclassed on the home front, as Juventus and AC Milan mopped up Italian trophy after Italian trophy.

MANCINI MAGIC

The turning point came with the appointment of current Manchester City boss Roberto Mancini, who brought silverware and respect back to Inter. The club won the Serie A league title again in 2006 as a result of first-placed team Juventus being stripped of points because of the match-fixing scandal that engulfed Italian football.

In recent seasons, Inter Milan – courtesy of that Champions League success – have become a force to be reckoned with once more.

While their sixth-place finish in Serie A in 2012 is below the level of expectation Inter supporters generally have for their club, there's a sense that the turnaround in Inter's fortunes is all but complete.

DID YOU KNOW?
Inter Milan are the world's 12th richest team, say Forbes – and Italy's third richest after AC Milan and Juventus

Full name **Arsenal Football Club** | Nickname **The Gunners** | Founded **1886** | Ground **Emirates Stadium** (60,432)

ARSENAL

The European (and domestic) trophy drought continues

CLUB FACTFILE

Club homepage
Arsenal.com

Rivals Tottenham

CL Seasons 14

QF appearances 6

SF appearances 2

Final appearances 1

CHAMPIONS LEAGUE ★ STAR

Thierry Henry

Appearances 380

1999-2007 and 2012 (loan)

Probably the most elegant footballer the English Premier League has seen. Like Ronnie O'Sullivan and Roger Federer, Thierry Henry was the kind of sportsman who made his craft look beautiful – a joy to watch. Arsène Wenger brought the Frenchman to north London from Juventus and convinced him he was a striker, not a winger – a scorer as well as a creator. Thereafter, Henry became the scourge/envy of every European manager crushing teams with guile, pace and a pulsating finish.

TROPHY HUNT

Where do Arsenal go from here? Since the appointment of Arsène Wenger as manager in 1996, the club have picked up a deserved reputation for playing stylish football and, for the most part, this has brought results to north London. Wenger has won the Premier League title three times with the Gunners, the last time in 2003/04, their undefeated 'Invincibles' season. He has also added four FA Cups to the club's trophy cabinet.

The problem is, success has dried up in recent seasons and rivals such as Chelsea and Manchester City have attracted billionaire investors to bolster their squads. Arsenal can't, and haven't, competed with that. In fact, they have suffered a continual loss of star players, with the likes of Cesc Fábregas and Robin van Persie among the big names to have questioned the club's ambition.

YOUNG GUNS

Wenger has pressed ahead with his youth-first policy and has brought through exciting new talent after exciting new talent at the Emirates. The problem is, when that talent reaches a certain point, they increasingly look to ply their trade elsewhere.

Arsenal still have the ability to pull out impressive results, though. The doom-mongers during the early part of the 2011/12 season had to eat their words after Arsenal rallied to finish third in the Premier League. And while they didn't end their trophy drought (the closest they have come is a 2011 League Cup final defeat by Birmingham City), the Gunners continue to perform.

DID YOU KNOW?

Arsenal were the first London club to get to the Champions League final, two years before Chelsea

CONSISTENCY

Arsenal are a regular bet to get past the Champions League group stages and, occasionally, they show the spark that suggests they may go all the way.

The closest they have come was in reaching the 2006 final, which they mostly played with 10 men after goalkeeper Jens Lehmann was sent off. Even so, Barcelona had to come from behind to secure a 2-1 victory. Arsenal were also semi-finalists in 2009 and quarter-finalists in 2010, and although they might not be the force they were, it would be unwise to write them off.

Full name **Association Sportive de Monaco FC** | Nickname **Les Rouge et Blanc (Red and Whites)** | Founded **1924** | Ground **Stade Louis II** (18,523)

MONACO

Crawling their way back from a financial abyss

CLUB FACTFILE

Club homepage
asm-fc.com

Rivals Inter OGC Nice

CL Seasons 6

QF appearances 3

SF appearances 3

Final appearances 1

CHAMPIONS LEAGUE ★STAR

Fernando Morientes

Appearances 28

2003-2004 (on loan)

A striker of some repute, Fernando Morientes's strength was his aerial prowess: he could guide the ball as accurately with his head as he could with his instep. His prolific scoring season helped Monaco to reach the semi-finals of the Champions League, with Real Madrid probably wondering why they'd loaned him out, nevermind let him play against them (Morientes scored the goal that knocked *Los Blancos* out at the quarter-final stage). One of the most complete marksmen of his era.

BUILT ON SAND

It would be no exaggeration to suggest Monaco's glory days look further away than they have ever been right now. Based in Monaco, but playing their football in France, the team finished eighth in the second tier of French football in 2011/12, having been relegated the year before.

Monaco's successes at the turn of the millennium – winning Ligue 1 in 1997 and 2000 – had, it seemed, been built on a financial house of cards and the club was tens of millions of euros in debt. The cost-cutting began in earnest around 2003 and while Monaco continued to punch above their weight for a while, the loss of big players took its toll.

AGAINST THE ODDS

Even so, as late as 2004 Monaco made it to the Champions League final, beating Chelsea and Real Madrid en route. They were foiled in Gelsenkirchen by Porto, who recorded a comprehensive 3-0 victory to take home the trophy.

But given the financial meltdown Monaco were facing, just getting to the final was an impressive achievement. It was the first time they had reached the final of Europe's premier club competition, although they had featured in the 1992 Cup Winners' Cup final, in which they were beaten 2-0 by Werder Bremen.

DID YOU KNOW?

Monaco's financial plight led to a ruling that they be relegated to Ligue 2, but this was overturned on appeal

FRESH START

At the end of 2011, the club was bought by new owners and there is a sense that Monaco have hit rock bottom and can start rebuilding. Although their fall has been relatively quick, they have a long road back.

Monaco have not played in European competition for half a decade, their longest absence since the 1970s, and given their current league position – and the recovering state of the club – it's going to be a while before that changes.

But Monaco have more pressing concerns. Financial stability and viability is the obvious priority – and they need manager Claudio Ranieri to get the team back into the top flight of French football at the earliest opportunity. Only then will Monaco be able to plot a return to European football.

Full name **Futebol Clube do Porto** | Nickname **Las Portistas** | Founded **1893** | Ground **Estádio do Dragão** (52,000)

PORTO

The giants of Portugal – and they're not bad in Europe either

★ **CL STAR**

■ **Deco** ■ **Appearances: 154** ■ **1999-2004**

A compact dynamo, Brazilian-born Deco was the little conjuror at the heart of the unexpected 2004 triumph.

DOMINATION

Perennial European performers, Porto are Portugal's most successful club side, boasting 26 domestic league titles and 16 cup wins. They have never been relegated from the top flight of Portuguese football and their dominance was demonstrated by the 21-point gap they had over their nearest rivals when claiming the 2011 league title. Porto are *the* team to beat in Portuguese football.

DID YOU KNOW?
Porto also have basketball, handball and motor racing teams, as well as their own insurance company

JOSÉ...

Having already tasted some success in European football, Porto were to achieve two of their biggest nights on the continental stage after the arrival of 39-year old José Mourinho in 2002. Within two years, he had guided them to victory in the UEFA Cup (2003), and the Champions League (2004). Porto haven't fared quite so well since, but they added the Europa League trophy to their sizeable collection in 2011.

20 something: The official titles of Porto city are: *Antiga, Mui Nobre, Sempre Leal e Invicta* (ancient, very noble, always loyal and undefeated)

CLUB FACTFILE

Club homepage fcporto.pt

Rivals Benfica, Sporting

CL Seasons 16

QF appearances 6*

SF appearances 2

Final appearances 1

*INCLUDES REACHING THE FINAL GROUP STAGE OF 92/93, EQUIVALENT TO QF

Full name **Olympique de Marseille** | Nickname **Les Phocéens** | Founded **1899** | Ground **Stade Vélodrome** (60,031)

MARSEILLE

First Champions League winners have yet to rediscover a winning formula

BUMPY RIDE

Tenth in Ligue 1 in 2011/12 was well below expectations for Marseille, who were French champions in 2010. But it's been a bumpy few years for the club. Stripped of the 1993 league title after a match-fixing investigation, Marseille have had an 'always the bridesmaid' element to them over the past decade. That said, many quality players have passed through the Stade Vélodrome in that time.

DID YOU KNOW?
Marseille were the first – and, to date, the only – French team to win the Champions League

FRENCH FIRST

Marseille couldn't have made a better start in the Champions League, lifting the inaugural trophy with a 1-0 win over AC Milan in 1993. But since then, the best they have managed is a quarter-final appearance in 2011/12. They have done better in other European competitions, winning the Intertoto Cup in 2005 and reaching the UEFA Cup final in 1999 and 2004. The current Marseille side are some way off matching that, though.

★ **CL STAR**

■ **Basile Boli** ■ **Appearances: 163** ■ **1990-1994**

A mega-hard, enigmatic defender who rose to score the decisive header in the inaugural Champions Lague final.

CLUB FACTFILE

Club homepage om.net

Rivals PSG

CL Seasons 8

QF appearances 2

SF appearances 1

Final appearances 1

20 something: Club motto *Droit Au But* ('Straight to the Goal') and a Champions League victory star border the badge on Marseille's kit

Full name **Ballspiel-Verein Borussia 1909 eV Dortmund** | Nickname **Die Borussen (Borussians)** | Founded **1909** | Ground **Signal Iduna Park** (81,264)

BORUSSIA DORTMUND

The German champions looking for some renewed European bite

TOP DOGS

Reigning German champions Borussia Dortmund may not quite be at the level that they were in the 1990s, but their young team (and the club have developed many of its own players) show promise. Borussia Dortmund have the potential to enjoy a new golden era under Jürgen Klopp, who has brought new success since his appointment as manager in 2009. Catching them is going to take some doing.

DID YOU KNOW?
Borussia Dortmund's ground, Signal Iduna Park, is Germany's largest stadium, with a capacity of more than 80,000

CHEQUERED

Borussia Dortmund knocked three goals past Juventus, with one in reply, to secure the Champions League trophy in 1997. Since then – aside from runners-up spot in the UEFA Cup five years later – Dortmund have struggled, often not even qualifying for the Champions League. Four defeats in six group-stage games in 2011/12 suggests their domestic form hasn't translated to Europe, but most pundits expect better from them this time around.

★ CL STAR

■ **Andreas Möller** ■ **Apps: 228** ■ **1988-90 & 1994-00**

With an enviable goal tally for a midfielder, Möller's big-stage presence marked him out across Europe as a dangerous man.

CLUB FACTFILE

Club homepage
bvb.de

Rivals Bayern Munich

CL Seasons 7

QF appearances 2

SF appearances 2

Final appearances 1

20 something: Rather bizarrely, Borussia Dortmund's club motto is *Echte Liebe*, 'True Love'

Full name **Valencia Club de Fútbol** | Nickname **Los Che** | Founded **1919** | Ground **Mestalla** (55,000)

VALENCIA

The Spanish contenders who don't play in El Clásico

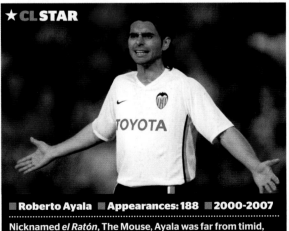

★ CL STAR

■ **Roberto Ayala** ■ **Appearances: 188** ■ **2000-2007**

Nicknamed *el Ratón*, The Mouse, Ayala was far from timid, being one of the most dominant defenders of his generation.

UNDERDOGS

Playing in the shadows of Catalan and capital giants Barcelona and Real Madrid means Valencia's trophy cabinet isn't troubled too often, although two La Liga titles under manager Rafa Benítez are highlights of the past decade. In 2011/12, though, third-placed Valencia were 39 points behind champions Real Madrid. Regular Champions League football continues to entertain the crowds at Mestalla, however.

DID YOU KNOW?
Valencia have been blighted by debt in recent years, leading to the sale of Juan Mata, David Silva and David Villa

SO NEAR...

Valencia have the unenviable record of losing consecutive Champions League finals – 3-0 to Real Madrid in 2000 and 5-4 on penalties to Bayern Munich in 2001. Their European trophies are sparse, with a Cup Winners' Cup, two Super Cups and, more recently, a Europa League triumph in 2004. In three of their past five Champions League appearances, Valencia have failed to get out of the group stages.

CLUB FACTFILE

Club homepage
valenciacf.com

Rivals Levante UD

CL Seasons 8

QF appearances 4

SF appearances 2

Final appearances 2

20 something: Despite financial difficulties, construction is under way in Valencia on a new 75,000-seater stadium, Nou Mestalla

Full name **Bayer 04 Leverkusen** | Nickname **Werkself (Factory Squad)** | Founded **1904** | Ground **BayArena** (30,210)

BAYER LEVERKUSEN

The team that rues the day they ever met Zinedine Zidane

★ CL STAR

■ Ze Roberto ■ Appearances: 113 ■ 1998-2002

Endeared himself to the fans with his indomitable spirit and played a major role in *Werkself*'s most lauded, decorated era.

CLOSE, NO CIGAR

Despite living in the shadow of Bayern Munich, Bayer Leverkusen have managed a few successes of their own, including the UEFA Cup in 1988. But, too often, the club falls just short. They have been second in the Bundesliga five times in the past 15 years, without ever winning it. Leverkusen have also worked their way through a fair few managers, but recently seem to be on an upward path.

DID YOU KNOW?
Bayer Leverkusen are owned by drugs company Bayer AG, much to the amusement of rival fans

ZIDANE STRIKES

Bayer Leverkusen have a good Champions League record and, although they have never won the trophy, they are not just in it to make up the numbers. They reached the final in 2002, but lost 2-1 to Real Madrid at Hampden Park thanks to an early strike from Raúl and a stunning volleyed goal by Zinedine Zidane just before half-time. But Leverkusen regularly progress from the group stages of whichever European Cup they are in.

CLUB FACTFILE

Club homepage bayer04.de

Rivals Bayern Munich

CL Seasons 7

QF appearances 2

SF appearances 1

Final appearances 1

20 something: In the summer of 2002, Leverkusen lost Michael Ballack and Ze Roberto to their arch-rivals, Bayern Munich

---

Full name **Olympique Lyonnais** | Nickname **Les Gones (The Kids)** | Founded **1899** | Ground **Stade de Gerland** (40,500)

LYON

A decade to remember at home, but European travels draw a blank

SEVEN UP

French football will have to wait a long, long time for a club to repeat Lyon's achievements of the past decade. Built on very solid foundations, they won their first Ligue 1 title in 2002 – an achievement that kickstarted a run of seven straight league championships. In 2008, Lyon won the French domestic double for the first time, too. It was a fabulous era, broken only by Bordeaux winning the title in 2009.

DID YOU KNOW?
Olympique Lyonnais were formed in 1950 after rows in original club Lyon Olympique Universitaire

EMPTY HANDED

European success, outside of an Intertoto Cup win in 1997, has eluded Lyon and their Champions League form has been patchy. Three consecutive quarter-final appearances from 2004 to 2006, and a semi-final place in 2010, are as good as it gets and the French side have struggled to really break into Europe's elite. But they are always a threat and, at the very least, usually get out of the group stages.

★ CL STAR

■ Gregory Coupet ■ Apps: 518 ■ 1997-2008

A safe pair of hands for *Les Gones* for more than 10 years, a period in which Lyon have dominated French football.

CLUB FACTFILE

Club homepage olweb.fr

Rivals St Etienne

CL Seasons 12

QF appearances 4

SF appearances 1

Final appearances 0

20 something: Lyon's new €250m, 61,556-seater stadium, which at the moment is referred to as OL Land, will be ready in 2013

Full name **Philips Sport Vereniging NV** | Nickname **Boeren (Peasants)** | Founded **1913** | Ground **Philips Stadion** (35,000)

PSV EINDHOVEN

They peaked in the 80s, but still enjoy a modicum of success...

SLOW GOING

For a club with a history as proud as PSV's, the past three years have been uncharacteristically lean. One domestic cup aside, the club haven't finished in the top two in the Eredivisie since winning the title in 2008 (the last of four consecutive championship wins). PSV have had some excellent teams over the past 30 years, but a talent drain to other countries has taken its toll, particularly in Europe.

DID YOU KNOW?
When PSV won the European Cup in 1988, they did so without winning any of their last five games in open play

HIGH POINT

The pinnacle of Eindhoven's achievements to date came in 1988, when they beat Benfica 6-5 on penalties in the final of the European Cup. It was the club's second European prize, having lifted the UEFA Cup in 1978 after beating French side Bastia 3-0 in the two-leg final. More recently, PSV Eindhoven reached the semi-finals of the Champions League in 2005, but were beaten by AC Milan on the 'away goals' rule.

★ CL STAR

■ **Alex** ■ **Appearances: 84** ■ **2004-2007 (loan)**

A powerhouse of a defender who could intimidate strikers and pose a real threat from dead-ball situations.

*INCLUDES REACHING THE FINAL GROUP STAGE OF 92/93, EQUIVALENT TO QF

CLUB FACTFILE

Club homepage
psv.nl

Rivals Ajax

CL Seasons 13

QF appearances 3*

SF appearances 1

Final appearances 0

20 something: Bobby Robson won two Eridivisie titles in two years at PSV, but was moved on because of his perceived failures in Europe

---

Full name **Real Club Deportivo de La Coruña SAD** | Nickname **Depor** | Founded **1906** | Ground **Riazor** (34,600)

DEPORTIVO

One of the finest footballing sides in Spain might be on the way back up

★ CL STAR

■ **Roy Makaay** ■ **Appearances: 133** ■ **1999-2003**

A somewhat under-rated Dutch striker, who bagged a tonne of goals for Depor and won the admiration of the continent.

BOUNCING BACK?

Deportivo La Coruña's relegation from the top flight of Spanish football in 2011 – little more than a decade after they won the title – brought to an end one of the most exhilarating eras the club have ever enjoyed. Granted, they bounced back to La Liga in one season, but it will take some time to build a side that is again capable of regular top-three finishes and of lifting the Copa del Rey, as Deportivo did in 2002.

DID YOU KNOW?
Between 1999 and 2004, Deportivo were regarded as one of the best teams Spanish football had seen

PROUD RECORD

Considering the comparatively small city in which Deportivo is based, their European achievements are something to be proud of. To date, the peak of their Champions League performances came in 2004, when they reached the semi-finals of the tournament, losing to a single penalty kick over two legs to eventual tournament winners Porto. An Intertoto Cup victory in 2008 is Deportivo's sole European trophy to date.

CLUB FACTFILE

Club homepage
canaldeportivo.com

Rivals Celta Vigo

CL Seasons 5

QF appearances 3

SF appearances 1

Final appearances 0

20 something: Deportivo v Celta Vigo matches are known as Galician derbies. Deportivo have a record 25 victories in the meets

Bayern enjoyed voracious home
support in Munich's Allianz Arena
– nicknamed the *Schlauchboot*
(inflatable boat) – as they
attempted to win a fifth European
Cup title in 2011/12. But Chelsea
held off their waves of attacks to
win the trophy 4-3 on penalties.

Full name **Football Club Dynamo Kyiv** | Nickname **Bilo-Syni (White-Blues)** | Founded **1927** | Ground **Olimpiysky National Sports Complex** (70,500)

DYNAMO KYIV

Dominators of Ukrainian football, but perennial strugglers in Europe

★ CL STAR

- **Serhiy Rebrov** ■ **Apps: 242** ■ **1992-00 & 2005-08**

The yin to Andriy Shevchenko's yang, Rebrov is the highest scorer in the history of the Ukrainian Premier League.

GIANTS

Before and since the collapse of the Soviet empire, Dynamo Kyiv have been a force to be reckoned with. A record 13 league titles between 1961 and 1990, plus a bevy of cup wins, made them the team to beat in the USSR – and it was business as usual after the creation of the Ukrainian Premier League. A further 13 titles followed, as well as a few runners-up spots, but they have not won the title since 2009.

DID YOU KNOW?

Dynamo Kyiv have never dropped below the top-flight in Soviet or in Ukrainian football

NOT GIANTS

Dynamo Kyiv have struggled in European competition in the modern era. The last of their two Cup Winners' Cup triumphs came in 1986 and they have not progressed past the group stages of the Champions League since 1999, when they reached the semi-finals for the only time, losing 4-3 on aggregate to Bayern Munich. They have fared better in the Europa League, but Dynamo Kyiv are still domestic giants, and European pretenders.

20 something: After the death of Valeriy Lobanovskyi in 2002, Dynamo Kyiv's stadium was renamed in honour of the legendary manager

CLUB FACTFILE

Club homepage fcdynamo.kiev.ua

Rivals Shakhtar

CL Seasons 19

QF appearances 2

SF appearances 1

Final appearances 0

Full name **Panathinaikos Athlitikos Omilos** | Nickname **To Trifylli (The Shamrock)** | Founded **1908** | Ground **Olympic Stadium** (69,618)

PANATHINAIKOS

Greek giants who need to put their sorry recent history behind them

POINTS PAIN

It's been a tough year for Panathinaikos. Having achieved the domestic double in 2010 and reached the last 16 of the Europa League, 2011/12 was a season to forget. They finished as runners-up in the Greek SuperLeague, but had three points deducted after rioting marred a derby with Olympiacos. As a result, the club's board quit *en masse* and a rebuilding exercise is now under way.

DID YOU KNOW?

Panathinaikos are the only Greek team to have gone a season unbeaten – 24 wins and six draws in 1963/64

GROUP HUG

There has been plenty of European football in Panathinaikos's history, but success has been harder to come by. The closest they have come to a trophy was reaching the 1971 European Cup final, but they lost 2-0 to Ajax. They also reached 1996 Champions League semi-finals, but were beaten by the same club. More recently, Panathinaikos occasionally master the group stages, but rarely go much further.

★ CL STAR

- **Krzysztof Warzycha** ■ **Apps: 390** ■ **1989-2004**

Scored 273 goals for the club during a 15-year tenure and is one of the best foreigners to have played in Greece.

CLUB FACTFILE

Club homepage pao.gr

Rivals Olympiacos

CL Seasons 12

QF appearances 2

SF appearances 1

Final appearances 0

20 something: Matches against Olympiacos are referred to as 'The Derby of the Eternal Enemies' (they don't like each other much)

Full name **Fußballclub Gelsenkirchen-Schalke 04 eV** | Nickname **Die Königsblauen (Royal Blues)** | Founded **1904** | Ground **Veltins Arena** (61,673)

SCHALKE 04

The beaten semi-finalists of 2011 return to the Champions League

PAST GLORIES

It has been more than half a century since the glory days of Schalke. They have not won the Bundesliga since 1958, but they are still regular contenders for domestic honours – two German cup victories in the past 10 years are testament to that. Schalke's attacking style of football has won them many admirers in recent years and secured them third place in the league in 2011/12, albeit 17 points off top spot.

DID YOU KNOW?
Schalke are currently managed by Dutchman Huub Stevens, who led the team to victory in the 1997 UEFA Cup

EURO SUCCESS

Schalke have enjoyed some solid European success, with Intertoto Cup wins in 2003 and 2004, and a 1997 UEFA Cup victory. But they were beaten 6-1 by Manchester United at the semi-final stage of the 2011 Champions League, having appeared in the 2008 quarter-finals. Schalke have spent more time in the UEFA Cup and Europa League than the Champions League, but are back in the premier competition for 2012/13.

★ **CL STAR**

■ **Klass-Jan Huntelaar** ■ **Apps: 56** ■ **2010-Present**

Spoken about with great reverence in Gelsenkirchen, Huntelaar scored 29 goals in the Bundesliga in 2011/12.

20 something: Schalke's mascot is called Erwin and derby matches against Dortmund are referred to in Germany as the 'Revierderby'

CLUB FACTFILE

Club homepage
schalke04.de

Rivals B Dortmund

CL Seasons 5

QF appearances 2

SF appearances 1

Final appearances 0

Full name **Villarreal Club de Fútbol SAD** | Nickname **El Submarino Amarillo (Yellow Submarine)** | Founded **1923** | Ground **El Madrigal** (24,890)

VILLAREAL

Relegated but still strong – and a penalty away from a possible Champions League final

★ **CL STAR**

■ **Diego Forlan** ■ **Appearances: 106** ■ **2004-2007**

What he failed to achieve at Manchester United he did in abundance at Villareal: scoring goals – and lots of them.

DOWN, NOT OUT?

With two minutes of the 2011/12 La Liga season to go, Villareal – a small team that punches above their weight – were safe from relegation. But a late goal by Atlético Madrid condemned them to the second tier. Their passionate fans remain behind the team, though – and with good reason: for a small side, Villareal have ben regular star performers in Spanish football and frequently qualify for Europe.

DID YOU KNOW?
Villareal have the nickname Yellow Submarine because of their bright yellow playing strip

MIXED FORTUNES

Villareal enjoyed Intertoto Cup wins in 2003 and '04, but have never quite done it in the Champions League. They have had their moments: the 2006 semi-final defeat by Arsenal, in which Juan Román Riquelme's last-minute penalty was saved, came after they had beaten Inter Milan and drawn with Manchester United. However, qualification has been far from assured recently and they were well beaten in the 2012 group stage.

CLUB FACTFILE

Club homepage
Villarealcf.es

Rivals Valencia

CL Seasons 4

QF appearances 2

SF appearances 1

Final appearances 0

20 something: In 2005/06 Villareal defeated Everton 4-2 on aggregate in a play-off for the Champions League group stages

Full name **Idrottsforeningen Kamraterna Goteborg** | Nickname **Blavitt (Blue-White)** | Founded **1904** | Ground **Gamla Ullevi** (18,800)

IFK GOTHENBURG

Effectively finished in the top-four in the Champions League's first season

★ CL STAR

■ **Hakan Mild** ■ **Apps: 246** ■ **1989-93+ (see below)**

Enjoyed four stints at the club he loved – the second from 1995-96, the third 1998 to 2001 and the fourth 2002 to 2005.

GIANT

Having been in the top flight of Swedish football since 1977, the longest continual run of any Allsporto venskan side, Gothenburg moved into their new stadium in 2009 – and haven't won a trophy since. Two league titles in a decade is seen as poor by IFK's high standards, with their last championship triumph coming in 2007. A seventh-place finish in 2011 was a particular disappointment to their fans.

SLEEPING

Gothenburg's finest hours in Europe have so far been in the 1980s, with UEFA Cup wins in '82 and '87. Although they effectively reached the semis in the inaugural season (they were second in the final Group B, behind Milan) and also the quarter-finals in 1995, when they lost on the 'away goals' rule to Bayern Munich, since then they've not got past the group stage and, in recent seasons, have struggled even to break into the Europa League.

DID YOU KNOW?
Sven-Goran Eriksson's second managerial job was at Gothenburg. He won the 1982 treble of league, cup and UEFA Cup

CLUB FACTFILE

Club homepage ifkgoteborg.se

Rivals Orgryte IS, GAIS

CL Seasons 6

QF appearances 1

SF appearances 1*

Final appearances 0

*CAME SECOND IN FINAL GROUP B BEHIND EVENTUAL RUNNERS-UP MILAN IN 1992/93

20 something: Whereas city rivals Orgryte are seen as a middle-class, even upper-class club, IFK are very much for the working classes

---

Full name **Paris Saint-Germain Football Club** | Nickname **PSG** | Founded **1919** | Ground **Parc des Princes** (48,712)

PARIS SAINT-GERMAIN

Is big money set to bring back the good times to the Parc des Princes?

OH LA LA

Success in domestic cup competitions (most recently in 2010) has masked problems at Paris Saint-Germain over the past decade. Flirtations with relegation and ownership issues have taken their toll on the former giants of France. But 2012 has offered fresh hope after PSG finished second in Ligue 1, their best performance for a while. With more stability, their dark days could be firmly in the past.

DID YOU KNOW?
PSG's transfer outlay in 2011/12 was a French record €108m, which helps explain their high league finish

90S NIGHTS

For PSG's finest European nights you have to go back to the 1990s. Their best performance in the Champions League was in 1995, when they were beaten in the semi-finals by AC Milan. But they only had to wait a year to secure European silverware, thanks to their Cup Winners' Cup triumph. But they have since failed to get past the knockout stage of the Champions League and fared only a little better in the Europa League.

★ CL STAR

■ **George Weah** ■ **Appearances: 96** ■ **1992-1995**

Named FIFA World Player of the Year, European Footballer of the Year and African Footballer of the Year in 1995.

CLUB FACTFILE

Club homepage psg.fr

Rivals Marseille

CL Seasons 4

QF appearances 1

SF appearances 1

Final appearances 0

20 something: *Allez Paris St-Germain*, sung to the tune of *Go West* by the Pet Shop Boys, is played before every match in the PdP

Full name **Leeds United Association Football Club** | Nickname **The Whites** | Founded **1919** | Ground **Elland Road** (39,460)

LEEDS UNITED

Glory hunting cost them dear, but they have one great night to remember

FALL FROM GRACE

Leeds United have paid a heavy price for chasing major glory. Little more than a decade ago, they finished third in the Premier League (having won the English title in 1992), and were enjoying European adventures. But financial problems resulted in a tumble down the English league pyramid and they remain outside of the top flight. However, there is a sense that this sleeping giant is about to awaken.

SAN SIRO NIGHTS

The Whites have played in the Champions League only twice. The first time they tumbled out quickly; the second time they had one of their most memorable cup runs of recent times. Leeds battled through to the semi-finals in 2001, at which point they were beaten by Valencia. But one of the highlights of their tournament was the celebrated 1-1 draw against AC Milan at the San Siro, which sent United into the knockout stages.

DID YOU KNOW?
Leeds reached the Champions League semi-finals while two of their players were facing a criminal court trial

★ CL STAR

■ **Dominic Matteo** ■ **Apps: 115** ■ **2000-2004**

Made his debut for the club against AC Milan, scored a pivotal goal in the San Siro and never looked back.

CLUB FACTFILE

Club homepage
leedsunited.com

Rivals Man Utd

CL Seasons 2

QF appearances 1

SF appearances 1

Final appearances 0

20 something: Don Revie, Leeds' most famous manager, introduced the all-white kit in 1961 to try to mirror the mighty Real Madrid

---

Full name **Rangers Football Club** | Nickname **The Gers** | Founded **1873** | Ground **Ibrox** (51,082)

RANGERS

Effectively top-four finishers in inaugural competition, but struggling now

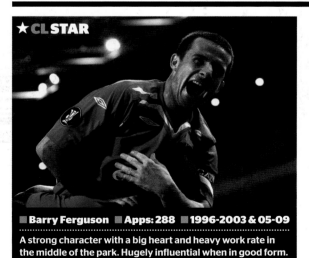

★ CL STAR

■ **Barry Ferguson** ■ **Apps: 288** ■ **1996-2003 & 05-09**

A strong character with a big heart and heavy work rate in the middle of the park. Hugely influential when in good form.

ROCK BOTTOM

It's hard to think of darker days for Rangers, who will kick off the 2012/13 season in the bottom tier of Scottish football because of their off-field financial problems. It'll be some time before they are competing for the Scottish Premier League title again, but there's a sense that Rangers have hit rock bottom and can rebuild – and the day when they rekindle their on-field rivalry with Celtic will thus come with added fire.

DID YOU KNOW?
Zenit, who beat Rangers in the 2008 UEFA Cup final, were managed by former Rangers boss Dick Advocaat

FINAL FRIENDS

Given the budgets and reputations of the teams they beat along the way, Glasgow Rangers' journey to the 2008 UEFA Cup final was a major achievement. They lost against Zenit St Petersburg – and so failed to add to their only European trophy to date, the 1972 Cup Winners' Cup – but they won many friends along the way. In the Champions League, the best Rangers have managed is second in the final group of 1992/93, equivalent to a semi.

*CAME SECOND IN FINAL GROUP A BEHIND EVENTUAL WINNERS MARSEILLE IN 1992/93

CLUB FACTFILE

Club homepage
rangers.co.uk

Rivals Celtic

CL Seasons 17

QF appearances 1

SF appearances 1*

Final appearances 0

20 something: Rangers were named after an English rugby club by founders Moses & Peter McNeil, Peter Campbell and William McBeath

Full name **Football Club de Nantes** | Nickname **Les Canaris (The Canaries)** | Founded **1943** | Ground **Stade de la Beaujoire** (38,285)

NANTES

Canaries showing few signs of flying high in Europe again

★ CL STAR

■ **Nicolas Ouédec** ■ **Apps: 150** ■ **1989-1996**

Scored five times in Nantes' improbable 1995/96 Champions League run to become something of a club legend.

QUIET TIME

Currently in the second tier of French football and showing few obvious signs of lifting themselves back into Ligue 1, it has been a quiet couple of years for Nantes. Attendances are down and the overhaul of the club that took place three or four years ago has had limited positive impact. It's all a far cry from 2001, when Nantes were crowned champions of French football to claim the eighth and most recent league title.

DID YOU KNOW?
Nantes have had 11 managers in five years, with many more assistant managers coming and going, too

EARLY PROMISE

In line with other French teams, Nantes' finest Champions League days are to be found in the competition's infancy. In 1996, a 4-3 semi-final defeat by Juventus brought to an end Nantes' impressive run in the tournament. The club's tumble down the domestic leagues has limited their Champions League appearances to just one since then, in 2002 – and that situation doesn't look like changing any time soon.

20 something: Nantes are famous for their *jeu à la nantaise*, a revered collective spirit and attacking style of play

CLUB FACTFILE

Club homepage fcnantes.com

Rivals Stade Rennais

CL Seasons 2

QF appearances 1

SF appearances 1

Final appearances 0

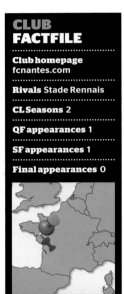

Full name **Sport Lisboa e Benfica** | Nickname **Benfiquistas Aguias** (Eagles) | Founded **1904** | Ground **Estádio da Luz** (65,647)

BENFICA

Still some way off their glorious best, but always competitive

60S REVIVAL?

Benfica may have enjoyed their finest days in the 1960s, but the club have long been linked with success. They have 32 Portuguese league titles to their name and their influence is felt way beyond Lisbon. The club have come through a difficult past 15 years and are now closer to resembling the Benfica of old. There's still some way to go, but claiming a league title in 2010 was a big step in the right direction.

DID YOU KNOW?
Benfica are not just a football club. They also have archery, table tennis, billiards, cycling and judo teams

DOUBLE TAKE

In its previous incarnation as a straight knock-out competition, Benfica were one of the very few teams to achieve back-to-back wins in Europe's premier club trophy, in 1961 and 1962. In addition, they were losing finalists twice in the next three years. More recently, the quarter-finals are as good as it has got for Benfica in the Champions League. They went a stage further in the Europa League in 2011, before being beaten on away goals by Braga.

★ CL STAR

■ **Joao Pinto** ■ **Apps: 220** ■ **1992-2000**

Part of the Portuguese 'Golden Generation' and a playmaker of some international standing during his days as an Eagle.

CLUB FACTFILE

Club homepage slbenfica.pt

Rivals Sporting Lisbon

CL Seasons 9

QF appearances 3

SF appearances 0

Final appearances 0

20 something: Benfica's greatest player is also their record appearance-maker and scorer: Eusebio, with 727 goals in 715 games

Full name **PFC Central Sports Club of Army Moscow** | Nickname **Koni (Horses)** | Founded **1911** | Ground **Arena Khimki** (18,636)

CSKA MOSCOW

A rich history, and new glories on the way?

SHARP SHOOTERS

With a heritage rooted in the Russian military, CSKA Moscow have always been regular contenders for honours. In the days of the Soviet Union, they survived relegations in the 1980s and then initially struggled in the new Russian league, before finally securing the title in 2003. Since then, CSKA have always finished among the top five and have added two further championships to their tally.

LONE STARS

Only one Russian side has won a European title – and CSKA Moscow hold that honour. They won the UEFA Cup in 2005, coming from behind to beat Sporting Lisbon 3-1 in the final. In the Champions League, their best performance has been a quarter-final spot in 2010, but there's a growing sense that CSKA are the kind of team you don't really want to be drawn against – especially when it comes to the away leg.

DID YOU KNOW?

CSKA stands for Central Sports Club of Army and Russia's ministry of defence is still a shareholder in the club

★ CL STAR

■ **Vagner Love** ■ **Apps: 158** ■ **2004-11**

Fast, tricky, loud and lithe, Vagner Silva de Souza scored one goal every two games during his time in Moscow.

CLUB FACTFILE

Club homepage pfc-cska.com

Rivals Dynamo Moscow

CL Seasons 8

QF appearances 2*

SF appearances 0

Final appearances 0

*INCLUDES REACHING THE FINAL GROUP STAGE OF 92/93, EQUIVALENT TO QF

20 something: CSKA Moscow's first training facilities were in Prince Yusupov's old stables, hence their nickname 'the Horses'

Full name **Associazione Sportiva Roma SpA** | Nickname **i Giallorossi (The Yellow-Reds)** | Founded **1927** | Ground **Stadio Olimpico** (72,698)

ROMA

One of Italy's best teams of the 80s, with sporadic sparks of life since

★ CL STAR

■ **Francesco Totti** ■ **Apps: 501** ■ **1992-Present**

The most complete, most revered, most successful, most written-about player in the history of the club. A true legend.

FLEETING FORCE

AS Roma were a force to be reckoned with in the 1980s, when they claimed a league title and four Coppa Italia victories. They were also one of the better teams in Europe, but it didn't last, although they still picked up the odd trophy, most notably their third league championship in 2001. More recently, new owners have come in and Roma's passionate fans will be hoping the glory days will be arriving again soon.

DID YOU KNOW?

Roma have only once topped their group in the Champions League, edging out Chelsea by one point in 2009

SPOT CHECKED

Penalty kicks denied Roma the European Cup in 1984, when Liverpool prevailed 4-2 in the shootout. Since then, they have reached the quarter-finals of the Champions League in 2007 and 2008, but gone no further. Likewise in the Europa League. Since losing the UEFA Cup final 2-1 to Inter in 1991, Roma haven't made it past the last eight of the competition. It seems their search for a first European crown will go on for a few years yet.

CLUB FACTFILE

Club homepage asroma.it

Rivals Lazio

CL Seasons 7

QF appearances 2

SF appearances 0

Final appearances 0

20 something: In 2016, Roma expect to move away from the Stadio Olimpico and into a new home, with seats closer to the pitch

Full name **Galatasaray Spor Kulubu** | Nickname **Cimbom** | Founded **1905** | Ground **Turk Telekom Arena** (52,695)

GALATASARAY

Turkey's only European winners are notoriously unwelcoming to visitors

★ CL STAR

■ **Hakan Sukur** ■ **Apps: 392** ■ **1992-95, 95-00, 03-08**

The 'Bull of the Bosphorous' was a beast in the air and is the scorer of the World Cup's fastest goal, playing for Turkey.

TOTAL CONTROL

It's 18 league titles and counting for Galatasaray, whose dominance of Turkish football has endured. They have enjoyed similar success in domestic cup competitions and hold the lion's share of Turkish football records too. As with most teams, they have had their ups and downs, but there's not a club in Turkey who wouldn't trade their footballing honours roll for Galatasaray's.

DID YOU KNOW?

When Galatasaray score a goal at home, *I Will Survive* by the **Hermes House Band** is played over the PA system

SOLO SUCCESS

As well as their many domestic successes, Galatasaray are also the only Turkish team to have won a European trophy. They lifted the UEFA Cup in 2000 after a 4-1 penalty shootout victory over Arsenal. A year later, they enjoyed another run in the Champions League, reaching the quarter-finals before losing 5-3 on aggregate to Real Madrid (they also came fourth in the final Group A of 1993/94, equivalent to a quarter-final berth).

CLUB FACTFILE

Club homepage galatasaray.org

Rivals Fenerbahce

CL Seasons 11

QF appearances 2*

SF appearances 0

Final appearances 0

*INCLUDES REACHING THE FINAL GROUP STAGE OF 93/94, EQUIVALENT TO QF

20 something: Galatasaray roughly translates as 'Gentlemen of Galata', though visitors to the TTA might have something to say about that

---

Full name **JSC Football Club Spartak-Moscow** | Nickname **Myaso** (The Meat) | Founded **1922** | Ground **Luzhniki Stadium** (84,735)

SPARTAK MOSCOW

In need of some gladiatorial spirit to revive their flagging fortunes

DOMINATING

Named after the gladiator slave Spartacus, Spartak Moscow had an iron grip on Russian football for the best part of a decade from 1992. During an incredible period of dominance, they won nine out of ten Russian league titles. In the past seven years they have also been runners-up five times. However, it has now been more than a decade since they brought the league title back to Moscow.

DID YOU KNOW?

Spartak have only been relegated from Russia's top division once, in 1976. They came straight back up

DISAPPOINTING

Since the Champions League came into being, it has been achievement enough for Spartak Moscow to escape the group stages. That is the best they have managed in virtually every season in which they have competed, save for a rare venture into the quarter-finals in 1996, after winning all six of their group games. Spartak lost that game 4-2 to Nantes and have not reached the latter stages of the tournament since.

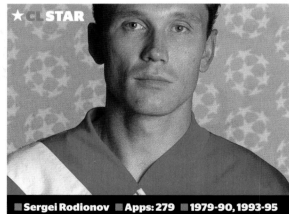

★ CL STAR

■ **Sergei Rodionov** ■ **Apps: 279** ■ **1979-90, 1993-95**

Scored some important goals for the most successful Spartak team in the modern era of European competition.

CLUB FACTFILE

Club homepage spartak.com

Rivals Dynamo Moscow

CL Seasons 13

QF appearances 2*

SF appearances 0

Final appearances 0

*INCLUDES REACHING THE FINAL GROUP STAGE OF 93/94, EQUIVALENT TO QF

20 something: Spartak Moscow's huge Luzhniki Stadium is one of the few major European, UEFA 5-star grounds with an artificial pitch

Full name **Athletikos Podosferikos Omilos Ellinon Lefkosias** | Nickname **Thrylos** (Legend) | Founded **1926** | Ground **GSP Stadium** (22,859)

APOEL

Domestic gods spring a surprise in Europe to give hope for the future

CABINET FEAT

As the most successful football team in Cypriot history, Apoel have no shortage of silverware. Few teams in Europe will have a trophy cabinet that is quite so heaving – 21 league titles, 19 Cypriot cups and 12 Super Cups. At least every other season, Apoel add a trophy to their collection and, while the 1980s were relatively lean years, the current side are formidable, domestically.

DID YOU KNOW?
APOEL did a league and cup double in 1996, and also went the whole season without being beaten in the league

SIGNS OF LIFE

Cyprus is hardly a powerhouse in international football, but Apoel have shown signs of significant life on the club scene. Usually first- or group-round fodder in European competitions, they sprung a real surprise in 2011/12 by making it to the Champions League quarter-final stage for the first time. Real Madrid swiftly disposed of them at that point, 8-2 on aggregate, but there was the sense that a real step forward had been taken.

★ **CL STAR**

■ **Gustavo Manduca** ■ **Apps: 51** ■ **2010-Present**

Brazilian used mainly as a left-winger who enjoyed *the* tournament of his career in the 2011/12 Champions League.

CLUB FACTFILE

Club homepage apoelfc.com

Rivals Omonia

CL Seasons 6

QF appearances 1

SF appearances 0

Final appearances 0

20something: In the second leg of their 2011/12 quarter-final against Real Madrid at the Bernabéu, Apoel scored twice – but still lost 5-2

Full name **Tottenham Hotspur Football Club** | Nickname **Spurs** | Founded **1882** | Ground **White Hart Lane** (36,240)

TOTTENHAM HOTSPUR

A breath of fresh air, blown out of the 2012/13 Champions League by Chelsea's win

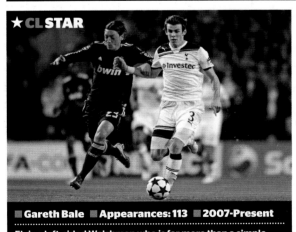

★ **CL STAR**

■ **Gareth Bale** ■ **Appearances: 113** ■ **2007-Present**

Flying left-sided Welshman who is far more than a simple kick-and-run winger. Coveted across the continent.

NEW DAWN

After years of playing exciting football with some success, it's an interesting time for Tottenham. Having missed out on Champions League football because Chelsea won the 2012 competition, Spurs dismissed Harry Redknapp and brought in André Villas-Boas. He inherits an exciting team, but will have quite a task to secure the English league title: Tottenham haven't won that since 1961.

DID YOU KNOW?
Spurs had qualified for the 2012/13 Champions League until London rivals Chelsea won the 2012 final

FRESH APPROACH

Tottenham have appeared in the Champions League just once, in 2010/11, but most commentators agree they were a breath of fresh air. After securing impressive wins against the likes of AC Milan (1-0) and Inter (3-1), they were beaten 4-0 in the quarter-finals by Real Madrid. Their European trophy cabinet isn't completely bare, though, with UEFA Cup victories in 1972 and 1984, and a Cup Winners' Cup triumph in 1963.

CLUB FACTFILE

Club homepage tottenhamhotspur.com

Rivals Arsenal

CL Seasons 1

QF appearances 1

SF appearances 0

Final appearances 0

20something: Spurs' early kit was dark blue, but was changed to white in the early 1900s in homage to double winners Preston NE

Acrobatics in the San Siro in
2004 by Brazilian maestro
Ricardo Izecson dos Santos
Leite, otherwise known as Kaká.
Another *Rossoneri* legend, Andriy
Shevchenko, scored the deciding
goal in this group game and Milan
went on to contest the final.

Full name **Football Club Shakhtar Donetsk** | Nickname **Hirnyky (Miners)** | Founded **1936** | Ground **Donbass Arena** (52,187)

SHAKHTAR DONETSK

One of the top two in Ukraine – and the only one with European silverware

★ STAR

■ Jadson ■ Apps: 173 ■ 2005-11

Man of the match in the last ever UEFA Cup final in 2009 and Shakhtar's playmaker for more than half a decade.

TWO OF A KIND

The current champions of Ukrainian football, Shakhtar Donetsk regularly go head-to-head with fierce rivals Dynamo Kyiv for the league title. It's all a far cry from their humble beginnings as a miners' team and it was 25 years before Shakhtar really came into their own, in the 1960s. Since the advent of the Ukrainian Premier League in 1991/92, Shakhtar have finished in the top two on 17 occasions, winning the title seven times.

DID YOU KNOW?
Shakhtar Donetsk are the only Ukrainian team to have ever won the UEFA Cup, beating Bremen 2-1 in 2009

FIRST AND LAST

Shakhtar Donetsk don't have a bad record in Europe. The highlight came in 2009, when they were the last team to win the UEFA Cup before its Europa League revamp. There are signs of progression in the Champions League, too, with a quarter-final appearance in 2011 their best run to date. However, it ended in a 6-1 aggregate thumping by that season's eventual champions, Barcelona.

CLUB FACTFILE

Club homepage shaktar.com

Rivals Dynamo Kiev

CL Seasons 12

QF appearances 1

SF appearances 0

Final appearances 0

20 something: The club has been called Stakhanovets (1936–46) and Shakhtyor (1946–92), but has been FC Shakhtar since 1992

Full name **FC des Girondins de Bordeaux** | Nickname **Les Marine et Blanc** (Navy and Whites) | Founded **1881** | Ground **Stade Chaban-Delmas** (34,263)

BORDEAUX

Signs of recovery in France, but still suffering from continental drift

ON THE UP?

If, of late, Bordeaux haven't quite recaptured the golden age that they enjoyed in the mid-1980s, they certainly give the impression of a team on the up. Three Ligue 1 titles between 1984 and 1987 marked the best period for the club, and they reclaimed the title as recently as 2009. But in the 2011/12 season they only just scraped into fifth place in the table to earn themselves a Europa League play-off spot by a single point.

DID YOU KNOW?
Since 2001, Bordeaux have been wholly owned by the French broadcasting company, M6

EURO STUTTER

Bordeaux won eight of their 10 games en route to the 2010 Champions League quarter-finals, before being edged out 3-2 by Lyon. It's their best performance in the competition to date and an Intertoto Cup win in 1995 remains their only trophy. A 1996 UEFA Cup final appearance suggested more were on the way, but Bordeaux were beaten 5-1 by Bayern Munich and have not reached the same level again.

★ CL STAR

■ Marouane Chamakh ■ Apps: 230 ■ 2002-10

Prolific in the air during his eight years at Bordeaux, Chamakh has yet to make such an impact in north London with Arsenal.

CLUB FACTFILE

Club homepage girondins.com

Rivals Stade Bordelais

CL Seasons 4

QF appearances 1

SF appearances 0

Final appearances 0

20 something: Girondins de Bordeaux was founded as a shooting and gymnastics club. Football wasn't introduced until 1910

Full name **Fenerbahce Spor Kulubu** | Nickname **Sarı Kanaryalar (Yellow Canaries)** | Founded **1907** | Ground **Sukru Saracoglu Stadium** (50,509)

FENERBAHCE

Turkish titles come thick and fast, but European joy is thin on the ground

OUT IN THE COLD

Turkish football is generally a three-way fight between Besiktas, Galatasaray and Fenerbahce, the latter two sharing the same number of league titles – 18 apiece. But Fenerbahce have recently been embroiled in the match-fixing scandal that engulfed Turkish football in 2011 and were, therefore, not allowed into the 2011/12 Champions League. They finished the 2012 Super Lig season nine points behind Galatasaray.

FEELING BLUE

It was eventual finalists Chelsea who brought Fenerbahce's best run in the Champions League to an end in 2008. The English side won their quarter-final clash 3-2 on aggregate and Fenerbahce have never looked like achieving the same level of progress since. A Cup Winners' Cup quarter-final appearance in 1964 had been the club's previous best performance in Europe and it will take some leap for them to be contenders in 2012/13.

DID YOU KNOW?
Fenerbahce have retired the No12 shirt, arguing that their supporters are always the team's 12th man

★ CL STAR

■ **Alex** ■ **Apps: 240** ■ **2004-Present**

Has an incredible 136-goal haul from attacking midfield including six in one match against Galatasaray.

CLUB FACTFILE

Club homepage
fenerbahce.org

Rivals Galatasaray

CL Seasons 9

QF appearances 1

SF appearances 0

Final appearances 0

20 something: Fenerbahce were the first sports club in Turkey to broadcast their own television channel in 2004, Fenerbahce TV

Full name **Società Sportiva Lazio SpA** | Nickname **Biancocelesti (White and Sky Blue)** | Founded **1900** | Ground **Stadio Olimpico** (72,698)

LAZIO

Reigning Cup Winners' Cup champions misfiring in modern Europe

★ CL STAR

■ **Simone Inzaghi** ■ **Apps: 129** ■ **1999-2010**

Scored nine goals in 11 CL games in 1999/2000, including four in one match against Marseille. Prolific stuff.

FROM B TO A

There's little question of when Lazio's golden era was. On the brink of relegation to Serie C a decade before, Lazio finished second in Serie A in 1995 and came close to winning the title before eventually being crowned champions of Italy in 2000. Financial problems burst their bubble, though, and involvement in the Italian match-fixing scandal didn't help. But they managed a top-four finish in 2011/12.

DID YOU KNOW?
SS Lazio's club colours are based on the Greek flag. Being a multisport club, they wanted to pay homage to the Olympics

ETERNAL REIGN

Lazio won the last Cup Winners' Cup final in 1999, beating Mallorca 2-1 before also beating Manchester United to win the Super Cup in the same year. That built on their appearance in the 1998 UEFA Cup final in which they were thumped 3-0 by Inter. The Champions League hasn't been so kind to Lazio, though, with a 2000 quarter-final appearance their best showing. They have not made it out of the group stages since.

CLUB FACTFILE

Club homepage
sslazio.it

Rivals AS Roma

CL Seasons 5

QF appearances 1

SF appearances 0

Final appearances 0

20 something: In addition to football, SS Lazio compete in more than 40 sports – the most of any sports association in the world

Full name **Fußball-Club Kaiserslautern eV** | Nickname **Die Roten Teufel** (The Red Devils) | Founded **1900** | Ground **Fritz-Walter-Stadion** (49,780)

KAISERSLAUTERN

Have had their ups and downs, and won't be worrying Europe for a while

★ CL STAR

■ **Jürgen Rische** ■ Apps: 108 ■ 1996-99

East German striker who scored four important goals to help his team clinch Group F in the 1998/99 Champions League.

YO-YO

Compared to many of their Bundesliga contemporaries, Kaiserslautern's trophy cabinet isn't all that impressive. Three league titles, the last in 1998, and a few cup wins is a modest, if solid, return. The club have bigger problems right now, though, having been relegated to the second tier of German football at the end of last season. After their last relegation, in 1996, they bounced back the next season, and won the title the one after.

DID YOU KNOW?
Fritz Walter played for Kaiserslautern for 22 years and scored 380 goals in just 411 games

SLIM PICKINGS

Kaiserslautern have no European silverware and have only once appeared in the modern Champions League. They didn't do badly, but a 6-0 quarter-final defeat by Bayern Munich finally ended their run. They have fared better in the UEFA Cup, reaching the semi-finals in 1981/82 and 2000/01, but they have not qualified for Europe since 2004, so offer no immediate threat.

CLUB FACTFILE

Club homepage
fck.de

Rivals Bayern Munich

CL Seasons 1

QF appearances 1

SF appearances 0

Final appearances 0

20 something: Kaiserslautern's stadium and the adjacent street are named after the club's most famous ambassador, Fritz Walter

---

Full name **Olympiacos Club of Fans of Piraeus** | Nickname **Erythrolefki (The Red-Whites)** | Founded **1925** | Ground **Karaiskakis Stadium** (32,115)

OLYMPIACOS

It's all Greek for Olympiacos as European trophies elude them

DOMINANT

No team in Greece has a record to match that of Olympiacos. The reigning champions of the Super League, Olympiacos have won the title 39 times (11 since the turn of the millennium) and have secured the Greek cup on 25 occasions. They have done the double 15 times. Theirs has been consistent success, too, only losing their stranglehold on the domestic game at the end of the 1980s and the first half of the 1990s.

DID YOU KNOW?
Olympiacos CFP also consists of basketball, volleyball, water polo, boxing, sailing and wrestling clubs, and more

FALLING SHORT

For all their dominance in Greece, Olympiacos have barely made a scratch on Europe. They regularly qualify, but rarely get further than the group stages and early knockout rounds. The best they have done is a quarter-final spot in 1999, when they were narrowly defeated 3-2 by Juventus, having been five minutes from victory. Since then, two appearances in the last 16 is as good as it has got for them.

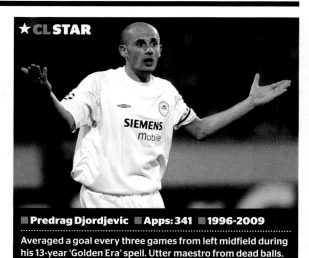

★ CL STAR

■ **Predrag Djordjevic** ■ Apps: 341 ■ 1996-2009

Averaged a goal every three games from left midfield during his 13-year 'Golden Era' spell. Utter maestro from dead balls.

CLUB FACTFILE

Club homepage
olympiacos.org

Rivals Panathinaikos

CL Seasons 14

QF appearances 1

SF appearances 0

Final appearances 0

20 something: The classic Olympiacos side of the 1930s had five Andrianopoulos brothers in the starting line-up

Full name **Club Atlético de Madrid SAD** | Nickname **Los Colchoneros (Mattress Makers)** | Founded **1903** | Ground **Estadio Vicente Calderón** (54,960)

ATLETICO MADRID

Overshadowed by their neighbours, but still enjoying days in the sun

MAGIC MOMENTS

Atlético Madrid have not qualified for the Champions League too often, but they have had their moments of success on the ultra-competitive Spanish stage. They did the Spanish double in 1996 – the last time they won either La Liga or the Copa del Rey – but they suffered relegation in 2000 and it took two seasons for Atlético to bounce back. But, of late, they have been a solid bet for a top-five finish in La Liga.

SILVER LININGS

They may not have enjoyed the success of their illustrious neighbours, Real Madrid, but Atlético Madrid are no slouches in Europe. They are the current UEFA Cup holders, having beaten Athletic Club 3-0 in the final, and also won the trophy in 2010, 2-1 against a courageous Fulham. In the Champions League, their best run has been to the quarter-finals in 1997, when they were beaten 4-3 on aggregate by Ajax.

DID YOU KNOW?
Atlético's most recent derby win over Madrid rivals Real in La Liga was in the 1999/2000 season, 3-1 at the Bernabéu

★ CL STAR

■ **Sergio Agüero** ■ **Apps: 175** ■ **2006-11**

Became the team's most important player at the age of just 19 and rarely failed to live up to his impressive billing.

20 something: Another team on the move, Atlético Madrid expect to be in their new 70,000-seater Estadio La Peineta in 2015

Full name **Association de la Jeunesse Auxerroise** | Nickname **AJA** | Founded **1905** | Ground **Stade de l'Abbé-Deschamps** (24,493)

AUXERRE

Having the same manager for almost half a century paid dividends

★ CL STAR

■ **Corentin Martins** ■ **Apps: 187** ■ **1991-96**

A critical part of Guy Roux's most successful Auxerre side, who regularly unlocked opposition defences.

GOING DOWN

The day in 1996 when Auxerre were crowned champions of France must seem like a long, long time ago after the club suffered relegation to Ligue 2 at the end of last season. They did the double that season, and added French cup wins in 2003 and 2005, but any hopes of a lasting dynasty were false. When manager Guy Roux – who led the club for more than 40 years in two spells – moved on in 2005, Auxerre's stability went, too.

DID YOU KNOW?
Guy Roux played for Auxerre from 1952 until he became manager in 1961. He stayed in post until 2005

QUARTERED

Two Intertoto Cup successes aside, Auxerre's best showing in Europe has been the quarter-finals of the Champions League in 1997, when they were stopped 4-1 by eventual tournament winners Borussia Dortmund. Their 2005 UEFA Cup campaign ended at the same stage thanks to a 4-2 defeat by CSKA Moscow. But Europe is on the backburner for Auxerre now, as they try to regain their Ligue 1 status.

20 something: Djibril Cissé, Laurent Blanc, Philippe Mexès, Basile Boli and Eric Cantona all came through the Auxerre ranks

Full name **Rosenborg Ballklub** | Nickname **Troillongan** (The Troll Kids) | Founded **1917** | Ground **Lerkendal Stadion** (21,166)

ROSENBORG

Norwegian kings haven't invaded Europe as often as their forebears

★ CL STAR

■ **Steffen Iversen** ■ **Apps: 193** ■ **1995-96, 2006-10+**

In his third spell at the club (2011-Present) for whom he can't stop scoring or winning titles. Still Rosenborg's main threat.

TOP TIPPEL

Norway has no more successful team than Rosenborg, a side who have won the Tippeligaen 22 times. But they have not been without their problems in recent years. For instance, in 2005 they were staring relegation in the face, but a late-season return to form saved them, and they have since added three more league titles to their honours board. However, they are not quite the dominant force in Norway that they once were.

DID YOU KNOW?
Rosenborg only went fully professional in the late 1980s after an injection of cash from their main sponsor

ONE HIT WONDER

Rosenborg have not really made an impact in Europe and their best Champions League campaign was in 1997. Then they faced Juventus in the quarter-finals, and held the Italian giants to a 1-1 draw in the home leg. But a 2-0 defeat in the reverse fixture ended Rosenborg's European dream. Of late, even getting past the group stages of European competitions has proved a step too far.

CLUB FACTFILE

Club homepage
rbk.no

Rivals Molde

CL Seasons 15

QF appearances 1

SF appearances 0

Final appearances 0

20 something: Rosenborg's record Champions League victory is their 6-0 thumping of Helsingborg in 2000

Full name **Legia Warszawa SA** | Nickname **Wojskowi** (Militarians) | Founded **1916** | Ground **Pepsi Arena** (31,800)

LEGIA WARSAW

The Polish army take to the football field but lack firepower in Europe

NEW HOME

Despite finishing third in last season's Ekstraklasa, Legia Warsaw were only three points from winning the Polish championship, in what was an incredibly close title race. They are not short of triumphs, though. Their last of eight titles came in 2006 and they have won the Polish cup for the past two seasons. Their 2012 victory was a good way to mark a season in which their stadium was completely revamped.

OLD STRUGGLES

Polish teams have often struggled in Europe and Legia Warsaw are no exception. Rarely seen in the Champions League, they reached the quarter-finals once, in 1996, when they were defeated 3-0 by Panathinaikos. Since then, they have mainly had to content themselves with UEFA Cup and Europa League appearances, but have never got past the early rounds. A European Cup semi-final in 1970 remains their best effort.

DID YOU KNOW?
Legia Warsaw became the Polish army's official club after being founded by soldiers during world war one

★ CL STAR

■ **Cezary Kucharski** ■ **Apps: 157** ■ **1995-97, 1997-99+**

Also played for the club in 2000-03 and 2005-06, presenting a goal threat every time he pulled on the jersey.

CLUB FACTFILE

Club homepage
legia.com

Rivals Polonia Warsaw

CL Seasons 4

QF appearances 1

SF appearances 0

Final appearances 0

20 something: Legia legend Cezary Kucharski now owns a sports management agency and is the sole agent of Robert Lewandowski

Full name **Hrvatski nogometni klub Hajduk Split** | Nickname **Bili (Whites)** | Founded **1911** | Ground **Stadion Poljud** (35,000)

HAJDUK SPLIT

Perennial Champions League strugglers enjoy home comforts

STILL WINNING

Hajduk Split had a better-than-average record before the disintegration of Yugoslavia. They won the league title nine times (the last one in 1979) and enjoyed several cup victories, too. The formation of the Croatian HNL at the start of the 1990s brought fresh success: Hajduk have secured six titles and, while they haven't topped the table since 2005, they remain regular championship contenders.

DID YOU KNOW?
Hajduk could not play in Europe in 1992/93 because UEFA did not recognise the Croatian Football Federation

UNQUALIFIED

Whether in the Champions League or the UEFA Cup/Europa League, Hajduk Split have struggled. Just getting past the qualifying rounds to the group stages has posed a serious challenge and the day they reached the quarter-finals of the Champions League, in 1995, seems a very long time ago. They were beaten 3-0 by eventual tournament winners Ajax on that occasion and they have made little progress since.w

★ CL STAR

■ **Tomislav Erceg** ■ **Apps: 160** ■ **1991-95, 97-98+**

Enjoyed five stints at the club (including 1999-00, 2001-02 and 2006) and scored lots of goals. A true journeyman.

20 something: In 1995, Hadjuk beat Steaua Bucharest and Anderlecht in Group C, but lost 3-0 to eventual winners Ajax in the quarters

CLUB FACTFILE

Club homepage hajduk.hr

Rivals Dinamo Zagreb

CL Seasons 6

QF appearances 1

SF appearances 0

Final appearances 0

Full name **Sportverein Werder Bremen von 1899 eV** | Nickname **Die Werderaner** (River Islanders) | Founded **1899** | Ground **Weserstadion** (42,500)

WERDER BREMEN

Double winners a decade ago but enduring mid-table mediocrity now

★ CL STAR

■ **Claudio Pizarro** ■ **Apps: 56** ■ **1999-01, 2008-09+**

Enjoyed another stint from 2009-12 and, despite signing for Bayern, is still revered by even the staunchest of fans.

FAIRLY MIDDLING

Werder Bremen have won the Bundesliga title on four occasions, most notably as part of a league and cup double in 2004. For some years afterwards, they were always in contention for honours, so their fans will have been disappointed with the team's 13th-place in 2011 and ninth place last season. Points-wise, Werder Bremen were closer to the relegation zone than the top five teams in German football in 2012.

DID YOU KNOW?
Bremen are allowed a single star on their kit in the Bundesliga in recognition of their four title wins

HISTORY DENIED

At one point, it looked as though Werder Bremen would win the last UEFA Cup before its Europa League rebrand. However, they lost the 2009 final 2-1 in extra time to Shakhtar Donetsk. Still, Bremen have tasted European success – a 1992 Cup Winners' Cup triumph and a 1998 Intertoto Cup win. The last 16 has been their best display in the current Champions League format, but Werder Bremen were European Cup quarter-finalists in 1989.

*INCLUDES REACHING THE FINAL GROUP STAGE OF 93/94, EQUIVALENT TO QF

CLUB FACTFILE

Club homepage werder.de

Rivals Hamburger SV

CL Seasons 7

QF appearances 1*

SF appearances 0

Final appearances 0

20 something: The Weserstadion is being renovated to add a third tier of seating and remove the track, so fans can be nearer the pitch

||||||||||||||||||||||||||||||||||||||||||||||||||||||||||||||||||||||||||||||||||||||||||||||||

Full name **Royal Sporting Club Anderlecht** | Nickname **Purple & White** | Founded **1908** | Ground **Constant Vanden Stock Stadion** (28,063)

ANDERLECHT

The best European team ever to come out of Belgium

★ CL STAR

■ **Par Zetterberg** ■ **Apps: 285** ■ **1989-91, 93-00, 03-06**

Gifted Swedish player who rarely played for the national team, but always did the business for Anderlecht.

HOME TRUTHS

Anderlecht are the current champions of the Belgian Pro League and have enjoyed no shortage of domestic success in the past. Last year's was their 31st title and they finished six points clear of runners-up Club Brugge. Their success has been consistent, without major peaks and troughs, and while their European fortunes have subsided, Anderlecht still have a very firm grip on matters closer to home.

DID YOU KNOW?
Anderlecht have been in Belgium's top league continuously since 1935. They have had four chairmen in that time

TRIPLE TRIUMPH

Belgium may not be a powerhouse of international football, but Anderlecht have had a surprising amount of success on the continent. Granted, their two Cup Winners' Cup and one UEFA Cup triumphs date back to the 1970s and 80s, but they are impressive achievements. In the modern Champions League era, they have never got past the group stage, but, in the old format, Anderlecht made the semi-finals in 1986.

CLUB FACTFILE

Club homepage rsca.be

Rivals Club Brugge

CL Seasons 13

QF appearances 1

SF appearances 0

Final appearances 0

20 something: In 1994, Anderlecht drew eventual winners AC Milan in the final CL group stage and refused to lose, twice drawing 0-0

||||||||||||||||||||||||||||||||||||||||||||||||||||||||||||||||||||||||||||||||||||||||||||||||

Full name **Club Brugge Koninklijke Voetbalvereniging** | Nickname **Blauw-Zwart (Blue-Black)** | Founded **1891** | Ground **Jan Breydelstadion** (29,472)

CLUB BRUGGE

The only Belgian team to get to the European Cup final

CUP KINGS

They can't rival the trophy room of Anderlecht, but Club Brugge have proved themselves in Belgian football over the years. They have been league champions 13 times, their last success coming in 2005, and are inching closer to regaining the crown after finishing as runners-up in the 2011/12 season. They have also won the Belgian cup 10 times, more than any other team, their most recent victory being in 2007.

DID YOU KNOW?
Only two English sides have won away to Club Brugges in Europe: Liverpool and Birmingham City

FIRST AT THE LAST

Club Brugge are the only Belgian side ever to have reached the European Cup final, which they managed to do in 1978. However, just as they had done in the two-leg 1976 UEFA Cup final, they lost to Liverpool, 1-0 at Wembley. Club Brugge's more recent European history has been patchy and when they have made it to the modern-day Champions League, they have never managed to get past the group stages.

★ CL STAR

■ **Franky Van der Elst** ■ **Apps: 462** ■ **1984-99**

A club legend, Van der Elst was an inspirational, tireless midfielder who played until he was 40 years old.

CLUB FACTFILE

Club homepage clubbrugge.be

Rivals Anderlecht

CL Seasons 7

QF appearances 1*

SF appearances 0

Final appearances 0

*INCLUDES REACHING THE FINAL GROUP STAGE OF 92/93, EQUIVALENT TO QF

20 something: The Blauw-Zwarts hold the record for the number of consecutive participations in the UEFA Cup, with 16

CHAMPIONS LEAGUE
STAR GAZING
....

Whilst flourishing at Real Madrid, it's obvious that playing second fiddle to Lionel Messi is beginning to grate on the young Portuguese prodigy. He'll need to help *Los Blancos* lift the Champions League in 2013 before he can win his Ballon d'Or back, though.

THE HISTORY

1992/93

Drama in gloriously branded abundance would stir the passions of a continent: favourites toppled, battles fought and scandals raged...

▼ DID YOU KNOW?

■ In 1991, controversial Marseille owner Bernard Tapie was suspended for a year by the French football authorities for his vitriolic behaviour from the touchline and for "injuring sporting morale" with his incessant haranguing of officials.
■ In AC Milan's first game of the group stage they crushed IFK Gothenburg 4-0, Marco van Basten scoring all four goals.

Tapie: served 8-month jail sentence in 1997

▼ TOP GOALSCORERS

Romário, PSV Eindhoven	7
Marco van Basten, AC Milan	6
Franck Sauzée, Marseille	6
Alen Boksic, Marseille	6
Johnny Ekstrom, IFK Goteborg	5

▼ ALSO IN 1992/93

■ **Ballon d'Or**
Marco van Basten (Milan)
■ **Mercury Music Prize**
Screamadelica
■ **BBC Sports Personality of the Year** Liz McColgan
■ **Oscar for best film**
Unforgiven

And so it began. At the behest of forward-thinking (some would say greedy) television types and Europe's most powerful club sides, the European Cup format was altered – for better or worse – forever, and the all-singing, all-dancing Champions League took its bow.

In a revolutionary UEFA congress meeting in 1991, a sharply suited, 35-strong panel had granted the competition full control of its television and commercial rights. A compact posse of multinational sponsors was gathered together – who would see their logos at every game, worldwide – while broadcasting rights were sold to each interested country. In the UK, these initially went solely to ITV, but later, more lucratively, the rights were sold to satellite broadcasters.

Encouraging the competition to move from a straight knockout format to phased group and knockout stages meant more lucrative clashes between the continent's greatest teams and more matches in which the carefully considered branding could be digested by fans.

But the initial format didn't prove successful for some of Spain's or England's biggest teams: Barcelona were dumped out of the pre-group, second-round knockout phase by CSKA Moscow and Leeds United were disposed of, rather efficiently, at the same stage by Ally McCoist and Glasgow Rangers. In fact, Leeds were lucky to even make it through the first knockout round. They had lost on away goals to Stuttgart, but won a rematch after it was discovered Christoph Daum, the Stuttgart coach, had fielded too many foreign players

38. FINALE
UM DEN POKAL DER EUROPÄISCHEN MEISTERVEREINE

OLYMPIQUE MARSEILLE – AC MAILAND
Mittwoch, 26. Mai 1993 · 20.15 Uhr

in the last eight minutes of the first-round encounter.

In the group phase, eight teams were split into two divisions, CSKA Moscow being the only representative from a preliminary round that had included refederated teams now split from the USSR and Yugoslavia.

AC Milan dominated Group B, winning all six of their games and only conceding one goal (scored by PSV Eindhoven's Romário) to propel themselves into the final at Munich's Olympiastadion.

Group A was a battle between Walter Smith's Rangers and Bernard Tapie's Marseille, still mourning 14 fans who died in Corsica after a stand collapsed during the semi-final of the subsequently cancelled French Cup. Neither side would lose a group match, but Marseille reached the final after they beat Club Brugge 1-0 and Rangers could only draw 0-0 at home to CSKA. Rangers have never again come close to reaching the latter stages of the Champions League.

Rangers lost out after the last group game, missing the final by a point. They have not come close to the latter stages of the Champions League again

▼ PLAYER OF THE TOURNAMENT

■ **Didier Deschamps, Marseille**
Exemplified the core spirit of Tapie's team. Strong in the tackle and rarely squandered possession in the middle of the park: Deschamps' unwavering grit helped Marseille to scale the continent's dizziest heights. He would go on to captain France during their 1998 World Cup and 2000 European Championship victories.

The youngest captain to lift the trophy, at 24

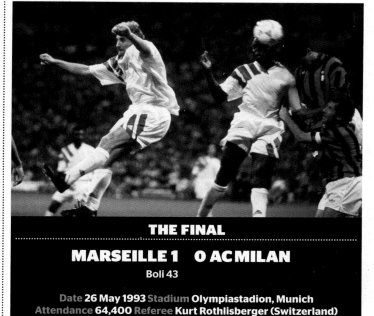

THE FINAL

MARSEILLE 1   0 AC MILAN
Boli 43

Date **26 May 1993** Stadium **Olympiastadion, Munich**
Attendance **64,400** Referee **Kurt Rothlisberger (Switzerland)**

The public relations disaster that was about to slap Bernard Tapie and his Marseille team right across the kisser tarnished a quite magnificent victory in Munich, full of heart and tenacity.

Fabio Capello had succeeded Arrigo Sacchi as manager of Milan and his side – including such rare delights as Franco Baresi, Frank Rijkaard, Paolo Maldini, Marco van Basten and new £13m, world-record signing Gianluigi Lentini – were considered the world's greatest team. But Marseille didn't care: AC Milan might have had the style, but the French side had the application and the appetite.

After soaking up Milan's early pressure, including two chances for Daniele Massaro, Marseille won a 43rd-minute corner. Abedi Pelé lofted in an outswinger and

strapping centre-back Basile Boli rose above Rijkaard to nod a deft header past Sebastiano Rossi.

Despite waves of Milan attacks in the second half, resolute defending and a bit of luck resulted in Marseille being crowned the first Champions League winners – and the first French club to lift the European Cup. Tapie was said by newspaper *Le Figaro* to have arrived back in the south of France after the victory "like a Roman general at the head of his legionnaires". Unfortunately, a multitude of match-fixing and bribery scandals involving Marseille erupted after the match, Tapie was sent to jail and Marseille were stripped of their Ligue 1 title, relegated and not allowed to defend their Champions League crown the following season.

THE LINE-UPS

Barthez, Angloma (Durand 62), Boli, Desailly, Eydelie, Pelé, Sauzée, Deschamps (c), Di Meco, Boksic, Völler (Thomas 79)

Rossi, Tassotti, Costacurta, Baresi (c), Maldini, Donadoni (Papin 58), Albertini, Rijkaard, Lentini, Van Basten (Eranio 86), Massaro

1993/94

Alex Ferguson put the hair dryer on charge, Cruyff's attacking spirit made the continent smile, but Fabio Capello enjoyed the last laugh...

▼ DID YOU KNOW?

■ Barcelona lost 1-3 to Dynamo Kyiv in the first round, but came back impressively in the second leg, winning 4-1 in the Nou Camp to qualify 5-4 on aggregate.

■ To reduce the number of 'dead' games at the end of the group stage, semi-finals were introduced in 1993/94, with the two leading teams in each group qualifying and the group winners having home advantage in the last four.

José Bakero scored two at Camp Nou against Kyiv

▼ TOP GOALSCORERS

Ronald Koeman, Barcelona	8
Wynton Rufer, Werder Bremen	8
Luc Nilis, Anderlecht	7
Hristo Stoichkov, Barcelona	7
Bernd Hobsch, Werder Bremen	5
Valery Karpin, Spartak Moscow	5

▼ ALSO IN 1993/94

■ **Ballon d'Or**
Hristo Stoichkov (Barcelona)

■ **Mercury Music Prize**
Suede

■ **BBC Sports Personality of the Year** Linford Christie

■ **Oscar for best film**
Schindler's List

At the same time as Europe's pre-eminent club competition was restructured in 1992/93, English football's top tier had been repackaged, initially as the Premiership and then the Premier League. Manchester United had manoeuvred themselves into the perfect spot to take commercial advantage of it, the Red Devils securing the inaugural Premier League title after 26 years in the wilderness, and were now expected to challenge the continent's elite.

But the fledgling Champions League was enduring a tough time. Inaugural winners Marseille had been barred from the competition for attempting to fix matches and Georgian club Dinamo Tbilisi were also removed from contention after allegations of bribery in their preliminary round match against Linfield FC turned out to be legit. There was certainly plenty of money to be made out of this wondrous new tournament, but at what price?

In the face of this PR disaster, UEFA pushed on – and so did the second Champions League tournament.

Sweeping political changes in Eastern Europe meant the competition was expanded to 42 teams – from the initial 16 – to include the champions of Estonia, Lithuania, Croatia, Slovakia, Latvia, Ukraine, Belarus, Moldova and Georgia. Twenty clubs featured in the preliminary round, and a further 22 joined in at the first-round stage, with two more knockout rounds reducing the number of clubs to eight for the group stage.

Glasgow Rangers, über-keen to make up for just missing out on the final in 1992/93, embarrassingly fell

at the first hurdle to Levski Sofia of Bulgaria, while Manchester United, shouldering so much expectation, lost on away goals in the second round to Galatasaray of Turkey.

Monaco, only in the tournament to replace Marseille and with Arsène Wenger at the helm, made it out of the group stage, but striker Jürgen Klinsmann couldn't propel them to the final. They finished second in Group A behind Barcelona, who were unbeaten in their six games and thus installed as favourites to win the competition.

AC Milan won Group B despite drawing four of their six matches, including two drab 0-0 stalemates with bottom side Anderlecht. Porto, who finished second, won one more game than the *Rossoneri*, including a 5-0 drubbing of German side Werder Bremen, but defeats in Anderlecht and Milan did for them.

In the newly introduced semi-finals, Barcelona beat Porto 3-0, while AC Milan overcame Monaco by the same scoreline.

Barcelona's brand of attacking football under Johan Cruyff was expected to gently unlock a wildly under-strength *Rossoneri*

THE FINAL

AC MILAN 4   0 BARCELONA

Massaro 22, 45,
Savicevic 47, Desailly 58

Date 18 May 1994 **Stadium** Olympic Stadium, Athens
Attendance 70,000 **Referee** Philip Don (England)

Considering the results in the buildup to the final, Barcelona were rightly favourites to win. Their brand of attacking football under the legendary Johan Cruyff was expected to gently unlock a *Rossoneri* bereft of Franco Baresi (suspended) and Marco van Basten (injured), with manager Fabio Capello also having to leave out Florin Raducioiu, Jean-Pierre Papin and Brian Laudrup because of UEFA's three non-nationals rule.

But the most feared strike partnership in Europe – Barcelona's Hristo Stoichkov and Romário – failed to shine in the Olympic Stadium, and it was one of Milan's foreigners, Dejan Savicevic, who took the spotlight, scoring with an incredible lob and setting up Milan's other three goals. Capello was reportedly

not a fan of Savicevic, but Milan's owner – newly elected prime minister of Italy, Silvio Berlusconi – had insisted he was in.

Daniele Massaro slotted home the first from a tight angle after a Savicevic run and cross, and benefited from another Savicevic raid to the byline for the second.

Savicevic scored the third and Desailly then powered through a gap in Barça's defence and on to Savicevic's pass to score a curling effort past Zubizarreta and become the first player to win the Champions League in consecutive years with different clubs. It was an unbelievable scoreline, but could have been more. Their revered Dutch trio of Ruud Gullit, Frank Rijkaard and Marco Van Basten had flown the nest, but Milan were as mighty as ever.

THE LINE-UPS

V

Rossi, Tassotti (c), Galli, Maldini (Nava 83), Panucci, Donadoni, Desailly, Albertini, Boban, Savicevic, Massaro

Zubizarreta, Ferrer, Koeman, Nadal, Sergi (Estebaranz 71), Begiristain (Eusebio 51), Guardiola, Amor, Bakero (c), Stoichkov, Romário

▼ PLAYER OF THE TOURNAMENT

■ **Paolo Maldini, AC Milan**
A wonderful servant to Milan for the whole of his career, Maldini was one of the best defenders of his generation, able to slot in at left-back or central defence. His impeccable positional sense meant he rarely needed to make tackles and it was this remarkable, almost psychic, footballing sense that elevated Maldini above his peers.

Maldini played 902 times for the *Rossoneri*

1994/95

An ultra-talented bevy of youngsters became the new Dutch masters of Europe – but Ajax's dominance would be short-lived

▼ DID YOU KNOW?

■ Milan were docked two points and ordered to play their remaining home games 300km from the San Siro after Salzburg keeper Otto Konrad was concussed by a half-full water bottle thrown from the crowd during Milan's 3-0 group win over the Austrian side.

■ The winning Ajax side had an average age of only 23, despite the presence in the team of 30-somethings Rijkaard and Blind.

Konrad was lucky it was only a plastic bottle

▼ TOP GOALSCORERS

George Weah, Paris St-Germain	**7**
Jari Litmanen, Ajax	**6**
Marco Simone, AC Milan	**4**

▼ ALSO IN 1994/95

■ **Ballon d'Or**
George Weah
(AC Milan)

■ **Mercury Music Prize**
Elegant Slumming

■ **BBC Sports Personality of the Year** Jonathan Edwards

■ **Oscar for best film**
Forrest Gump

Ah, the joys of being young! In 1994/95, a brilliant band of relative nippers from the football finishing schools of Amsterdam shocked an extremely experienced team to win on the biggest European stage. A wonderful sight indeed.

Their story begins with a major decision by UEFA – to no longer allow the champions of all European nations to compete in the Champions League. From now on, it would only include teams from the top 24 countries (as per the UEFA rankings), with the big seven footballing nations (Spain, England, Germany, Italy, Holland, Portugal and Russia) – plus the current champions – automatically entered into the group stage. This meant the biggest clubs would be guaranteed games and Europe's TV stations would have a guaranteed quota of matches involving their most popular and watchable teams. (After three years of this, smaller countries' champions were, quite rightly, re-admitted.)

The competition format changed to include four divisions of four teams each in the group phase, the top two from each one going through to contest two-legged quarter-finals.

Paris St-Germain eased through qualifying, 5-1 against Hungary's Vac, but Rangers were not nearly so efficient, losing 0-3 to AEK Athens.

Manchester United automatically went further in the Champions League than they had ever done before and were drawn against their previous nemesis Galatasaray, Barcelona and qualifiers IFK Gothenburg in the group stage. But their well-oiled Premier League machine didn't function so well on the continent and, despite

exacting revenge on Galatasaray, 4-0 at Old Trafford, they finished third behind the Catalans and the group-winning Swedes.

Paris St-Germain, with irresistible Liberian striker George Weah leading the line, were the only team to qualify from the group stage with a 100% record. But it was Group D's Ajax – with home and away wins over AC Milan – who were installed as the tournament favourites.

Despite winning at the Nou Camp and knocking out Barcelona 3-2 on aggregate in the quarter-finals, PSG met their match in the vastly experienced *Rossoneri*, losing 0-1 at home and 2-0 away.

Milan were joined in the final by their group-stage conquerors Ajax, after the Dutch side's thumping 5-2, second-leg victory over Bayern Munich in Amsterdam. Danny Blind handled the ball to give away the penalty for the Germans' second goal, but he wasn't sent off and went on to captain his team in the final.

This was something of a swansong for Ajax, their admired academy becoming a feeder for the might of Italy, Spain and England from now on

▼ **PLAYER OF THE TOURNAMENT**

■ **Frank Rijkaard, Ajax**
An unerring, thoroughbred talent, Rijkaard – alongside Danny Blind – formed the experienced and effective nucleus of the revamped Ajax side. A player and leader with rare vision, the 1994/95 final was to be his last game for the club he loved, and his influence and prowess helped to fashion a positive result for Ajax.

Rijkaard enjoyed the best send-off with Ajax

THE FINAL

AJAX 1   0 AC MILAN
Kluivert 84

**Date 24 May 1995 Stadium Ernst-Happel Stadion, Vienna
Attendance 46,500 Referee Ion Craciunescu (Romania)**

European heavyweights Ajax and AC Milan (playing in their third consecutive Champions League final) hadn't met at the business end of this competition since 1969, when Milan ran out 4-1 winners in the Bernabéu, inspired by their Ballon d'Or-winning playmaker, Gianni Rivera.

In front of 3,500 fewer fans in Vienna, the tables were turned by an Ajax squad that had taken the continent by storm – and, in particular, by 32-year-old midfielder Frank Rijkaard, who had scored the European Cup final winner for Milan in the same stadium five years earlier, against Benfica.

An experienced Milan dominated the first half, but had nothing to show for their efforts. Despite continuing to dominate in the second half, two astute

Ajax substitutions – Kanu for Seedorf and Kluivert for Litmanen – changed the course of the match. The rejigged Dutch side succeeded in opening up the game and Rijkaard's clever through pass set up Patrick Kluivert to grab the winning goal and, at 18 years 327 days, become the youngest scorer in a European Cup final.

What the world of football didn't know at the time was that this victory would be something of a swansong for Ajax. Their much-admired academy system would become less of a nursery for the Dutch club's first team than a feeder for the more financial might of Italy, Spain and England.

Within two years, the 1995 Champions League-winning side had disintegrated and none of the players were plying their trade in the Eridivisie.

THE LINE-UPS

Van der Sar, Reiziger, Blind (c),
F de Boer, R de Boer,
Seedorf (Kanu 53), Rijkaard,
Davids, George, Litmanen
(Kluivert 70), Overmars

Rossi, Panucci, Costacurta,
Baresi (c), Maldini, Donadoni,
Albertini, Desailly,
Boban (Lentini 84), Simone,
Massaro (Eranio 88)

1995/96

Italy's Old Lady sat Ajax's young bloods on her knee and taught them a lesson in holding one's nerve. They haven't reached a final since.

▼ DID YOU KNOW?

■ While Jean-Marc Bosman fought the European justice system, he lost his house and had two failed marriages.
■ Raúl became the youngest player to score a Champions League hat-trick (record now eclipsed by Wayne Rooney), in the 6-1 thrashing of Ferencvarosi.
■ Finland's Jari Litmanen is the only footballer to have played international matches in four different decades.

Bosman – won in court, but lost in love

▼ TOP GOALSCORERS

Jari Litmanen, Ajax	9
Alessandro Del Piero, Juventus	6
Raúl, Real Madrid	6
Krzysztof Warzycha, Panathinaikos	6
Patrick Kluivert, Ajax	5
Yuriy Nikiforov, Spartak Moscow	5
Nicolas Ouédec, Nantes	5
Fabrizio Ravanelli, Juventus	5

▼ ALSO IN 1995/96

■ **Ballon d'Or**
Matthias Sammer
(B Dortmund)
■ **Mercury Music Prize**
Dummy
■ **BBC Sports Personality of the Year** Jonathan Edwards
■ **Oscar for best film**
Braveheart

There was only one change to the format of Europe's premier club tournament for this season, but it was a significant one. A win in the group stages would now be worth three points, not two. It was a clear incentive from UEFA for teams to go for victory and spice up the early stages of the competition.

The main change to European football, though, didn't come via the game's governing body, but through a little-known Dutch player, Jean-Marc Bosman. In December 1995, a legal challenge made by Bosman in the European Court of Justice resulted in out-of-contract players aged 23 or above becoming free agents and able to move to other EU clubs for no fee, as part of the 'free movement' agreement within the European Union. Importantly for the Champions League, the court also ruled that regulations restricting the employment of EU citizens within member states was illegal. This was the start of player power, and there were plenty ready to place themselves in the shop window.

Allegations of bribery would again taint matches in the Champions League. Dynamo Kyiv, who fought through the preliminaries, beat Panathinaikos 1-0 in their first group game, but afterwards the referee, Lopez Nieto of Spain, disclosed a pre-match bribe of two fur coats and $30,000 by Dynamo representatives. The club were thrown out of the competition (to be replaced by Aalborg) and banned for three years.

Elsewhere, a 1-0 victory over Real Madrid showed champions Ajax – minus Frank Rijkaard – could still pack a punch and were not about to

give up their crown without a fight. Likewise, Juventus fans – having seen 'The Divine Ponytail', Roberto Baggio, sold to AC Milan – were taking great comfort from the emergence of a new star: Alessandro Del Piero. Their team finished top of Group C ahead of an increasingly competitive Borussia Dortmund. *Le Vecchia Signora* (The Old Lady) would go on to beat Real Madrid in the quarter-finals (a 2-0 home win rubbing out a 0-1 away defeat) and defeat a tricky Nantes side in the semi-finals, despite a nail-biting 3-2 defeat in La Beaujoire.

Under the guidance of Kenny Dalgish and with the bulging wallet of Jack Walker, Blackburn Rovers had momentarily dethroned Manchester United in the English Premier League, but failed miserably to emulate their domestic success in the group stages of the Champions League. They lost their opening fixture 0-1 at home to Spartak Moscow and never recovered, finishing bottom of Group B, a feat emulated by Rangers in Group C.

Juventus fans, having seen Roberto Baggio sold to AC Milan, were taking comfort in the emergence of a new star: Alessandro Del Piero

▼ PLAYER OF THE TOURNAMENT

■ **Gianluca Vialli, Juventus**
His frightening partnership with Roberto Mancini at Sampdoria was always going to prompt one of the big boys to swoop, and Juventus did just that in 1992. His last game for the club was as captain in the 1996 Champions League final. Edges out Ajax's Jari Litmanen as player of the tournament by virtue of his side lifting the trophy.

Vialli – decent right foot, divine goatee

THE FINAL

JUVENTUS 1   1 AJAX
Ravanelli 12   Litmanen 40
AET Juventus won 4-2 on penalties

Date **22 May 1996** Stadium **Stadio Olimpico, Rome**
Attendance **70,000** Referee **Manuel Díaz Vega (Spain)**

Juventus were seeking revenge after suffering defeat by Ajax in the 1973 final thanks to Rinus Michels, Johan Cruyff and their bevy of Total Footballers – and they wasted no time in doing so.

An uncharacteristic mix-up between Frank de Boer and Edwin van der Sar allowed the 'White Feather', Fabrizio Ravanelli, to shunt the ball home from the most acute angle to give the Italians the lead after only 12 minutes.

But Juventus couldn't hold on to their advantage – much like their keeper, Angelo Peruzzi, couldn't hold a tame inswinging free-kick by Frank de Boer. He spilled the ball into the path of prolific Finnish striker Jari Litmanen, who scored his ninth goal of the tournament with customary assurance.

The game ebbed and flowed for the rest of normal time and through both halves of extra time, which meant another final would be decided by a penalty shootout.

Edgar Davids' rather tame first effort for Ajax – followed by a succession of scores and a miss by Sunny Silooy – meant Serbian midfielder Vladimir Jugovic had the opportunity, with Juventus's fourth kick, to win the Champions League trophy. He kept his shot low and placed it well – to the keeper's right – and, despite 6ft 5in Dutchman Van der Sar guessing the correct way to dive, he could not prevent the goal.

Juventus had their retribution, winning only their second European Cup and their first under the competition's new banner of the Champions League.

THE LINE-UPS

V

Peruzzi, Torricelli, Ferrara, Vierchowod, Pessotto, Conte (Jugovic 44), Paulo Sousa (Di Livio 57), Deschamps, Ravanelli (Padovano 77), Vialli (c), Del Piero

Van der Sar, Silooy, Blind (c), F de Boer (Scholten 69), Bogarde, R de Boer (Wooter 90), Litmanen, Davids, George, Kanu, Musampa (Kluivert 46)

1996/97

She had her chance to defend the title, but the Old Lady looked a little old in the tooth, and the the Die Borussen took full advantage

▼ DID YOU KNOW?

■ Rosenborg capitalised on their Champions League returns of 1996/97, so much so in fact that, come 2005, they'd won the Norwegian title 13 years in a row.

■ Dortmund's victory signaled a clean sweep for German football: Matthias Sammer had been crowned European Footballer of the Year in 1996, they were European champions and fierce rivals Schalke had captured the UEFA Cup.

The 'Red Baron' was Dortmund's driving force

▼ TOP GOALSCORERS

Milinko Pantic, Atlético Madrid	5
Nicola Amoruso, Juventus	4
Artur, Porto	4
Alen Boksic, Juventus	4
Alessandro Del Piero, Juventus	4
Mário Jardel, Porto	4
Lars Ricken, Dortmund	4
(plus, 3 more players on 4 goals)	

▼ ALSO IN 1996/97

■ **Ballon d'Or**
Ronaldo
(Inter)

■ **Mercury Music Prize**
Different Class

■ **BBC Sports Personality of the Year** Damon Hill

■ **Oscar for best film**
The English Patient

After the Bosman ruling, which ended the limit on non-nationals in football teams within EU boundaries, foreign quotas rose dramatically at the start of the 1996/97 season, with most of the big teams increasing their pool of talent from across Europe.

Juventus recruited the French maestro Zinedine Zidane from Bordeaux to increase their tally to six; Manchester United's overseas count (not including UK and Ireland) rose from three to seven; and Borussia Dortmund increased theirs from six to 10, including former Juventus playmaker Paolo Sousa.

Enjoying the best spell in their history, the 1995/96 semi-finalists Panathinaikos were expected to make a similar impact this time around, but they lost the second leg of their qualifying match against Norwegian champions Rosenborg 3-0 to dramatically crash out.

Rapid Vienna comprehensively beat the reinstated Dynamo Kyiv (their ban was lifted by UEFA in April 1996 to "avoid hindering the development of football in Ukraine"), but the Austrians made little impact in the group stage. They weren't expected to, of course, and Group C favourites Juventus and Manchester United, went through in first and second position.

It was the first time Alex Ferguson's men had really asserted themselves in the competition and they cemented a new authority across the continent by thumping Porto 4-0 at Old Trafford in the quarter-finals – the first time a British team had reached this stage in more than a decade – with goals from Eric Cantona, Andy Cole, Ryan Giggs and David May.

Astonishingly, AC Milan lost their final group game 2-1 to Rosenborg, a 69th-minute winner from Liverpool-bound right-back Vegard Heggem enough to seal an incredible victory in the San Siro.

Patrick Kluivert's goal for Ajax was enough to beat Grasshoppers of Zurich in the final group games. But despite conquering Atlético Madrid 4-3 in a thrilling quarter-final clash, the Dutch side's notion of reaching a third consecutive final was snuffed out at the semi-final stage by holders, Juventus. The Italians won both legs, the second 4-1 in front of 70,000 baying fans in the Stadio delle Alpi.

Borussia Dortmund pulled off the same trick against Manchester United, winning 1-0 home and away against Ferguson's men – who were still adjusting to the rigours of playing on the continent. A Gary Pallister own goal did for the Red Devils in Dortmund and Lars Ricken's seventh-minute strike made the difference at Old Trafford.

THE FINAL

DORTMUND 3   1 JUVENTUS

Riedle 29, 34,   Del Piero 65
Ricken 71

Date 28 May 1997 **Stadium** Olimpiastadion, Munich
Attendance 65,000 **Referee** Sandor Puhl (Hungary)

Juventus, the trophy holders, had a stronger, more expansive, side this time around, which included the addition of Zinedine Zidane. Borussia Dortmund had the advantage of playing in their home country, but were not expected to cause the *Bianconeri* any major difficulties. In short, Juve were red-hot favourites – so it came as a huge shock when the Borussians conjured a 3-1 victory.

They took the lead with their first shot on target, Karl-Heinz Reidle striking after Juve failed to clear a corner. Riedle had apparently had a dream the night before that he would score twice and he managed it, heading home from another corner from Andreas Möller.

Alessandro Del Piero was brought into the fray after half-time by Juventus manager Marcelo Lippi and duly got the hard-pressing *Bianconeri* back into the game. But Dortmund's Lars Ricken, having only been on the pitch for 16 seconds, exquisitely lobbed a poorly positioned Angelo Peruzzi from 30 yards out to seal an unlikely victory. He also claimed the record for the fastest goal by a substitute in a Champions League final – a record unlikely ever to be broken.

The result also meant Paolo Sousa had made a point to his former employers: Juventus had placed the midfielder on the transfer list after he suffered what they believed was a career-threatening knee injury. But Borussia Dortmund gambled on the Portuguese playmaker and their boldness paid off in full.

Juventus had placed Paolo Sousa on the transfer list after he sustained a knee injury. Dortmund gambled on him and their boldness paid off

▼ PLAYER OF THE TOURNAMENT

■ **Zinedine Zidane, Juventus**
Despite twice suffering Champions League final defeats with Juventus, Zidane's skill and vision was unmatched in the competitions in which he played. As well as having an eye for intricate passes and delicate interplay, he could score precious goals. An all-rounder who would soon be recognised as one of the game's greats.

Zidane – lots of talent, not too much hair

THE LINE-UPS

Klos, Kohler, Sammer (c), Kree, Reuter, Lambert, Sousa, Heinrich, Möller (Zorc 89), Chapuisat (Ricken 70), Riedle (Herrlich 67)

Peruzzi (c), Porrini (Del Piero 46), Ferrara, Montero, Iuliano, Di Livio, Deschamps, Jugovic, Zidane, Vieri (Amoruso 73), Boksic (Tacchinardi 88)

1997/98

Juventus were being Lippi again but, come the end of the competition, it was Los Blancos who were shouting at the top of their voices

▼ DID YOU KNOW?

■ Before the Real Madrid v Dortmund semi-final, 'ultras' broke the crossbar of one of the goals. No spare could be found in the Bernabéu and they had to visit Real's training ground to find a replacement. The game was delayed for 45 minutes.
■ Dutch air traffic refused charter flights from Spain and Italy before the final – even the flight containing the Juve team! They eventually altered their stance.

Dortmund fans: dive bars, not crossbars

▼ TOP GOALSCORERS

Alessandro Del Piero, Juventus	10
Thierry Henry, Monaco	7
Filippo Inzaghi, Juventus	6
Serhiy Rebrov, Dynamo Kyiv	6
Andy Cole, Manchester United	5
Andriy Shevchenko, D Kyiv	5

▼ ALSO IN 1997/98

■ **Ballon d'Or**
Zinedine Zidane
(Juventus)
■ **Mercury Music Prize** Reprazent –
New Forms
■ **BBC Sports Personality of the Year** Greg Rusedski
■ **Oscar for best film**
Titanic

The most significant change to the Champions League took place before the 1997/98 tournament. Adapting the competition to suit various interested parties, UEFA greatly expanded the remit of the tournament and went against the very notion for which the competition is named. Yes, from July 1997 onwards you didn't necessarily have to be a 'champion' to qualify for the Champions League.

UEFA wanted to admit league runners-up from the top eight nations in its coefficient table and so they expanded the number of groups to six, with the group winners, plus the two best runners-up, reaching the quarter-final stage.

The domestic league runners-up who were admitted to the 1997/98 Champions League included Barcelona, Newcastle United, Bayer Leverkusen, Feyenoord, Parma, Paris St-Germain, Sporting and Besiktas. However, because Borussia Dortmund were awarded a direct seeding as champions, Galatasaray and Besiktas – champions and runners-up of Turkey respectively – were demoted to the preliminary round. Both got through to the group phase, but only one of the newly entered runners-up managed to break through to the quarter-finals: Bayer Leverkusen. The wheat appeared to be separating from the chaff, just as UEFA would have wanted.

Alongside the holders, Borussia Dortmund, and the mighty Bayern Munich, Leverkusen's presence took the total number of German clubs in the last eight to three, another signifier of their dominance of the era.

Dynamo Kyiv and Manchester United qualified for the knockout

phase earlier than most, but Real Madrid had to wait until the last group match – and a tense, if resounding, 4-0 victory over Porto – to go through, Croatian striker Davor Suker scoring two goals for the Spanish team.

Juventus left it till the dying minutes to qualify as one of the best runners-up after Filippo Inzaghi scored a precious winner against Manchester United in the Stadio delle Alpi.

Typically, the *Bianconeri* did not hang about in the knockout phase of the competition, beating Dynamo Kyiv 4-1 in their own backyard to claim a 5-2 aggregate win and then entertainingly dismantling Jean Tigana's Monaco side 6-4 on aggregate in the semi-finals.

On the other side of the draw, Real Madrid eased past an out-of-their-depth Leverkusen 4-1 and then rather undramatically knocked out the holders, Dortmund, 2-0 on aggregate, Fernando Morientes and Christian Karembeu scored the decisive goals in the Bernabéu.

With eight nationalities in their team for the final, Real Madrid's tradition of buying the best to be the best was re-emerging to great effect

■ **Raúl González, Real Madrid**
Not your typical line-leader, Raúl González had many more elegant attributes than brute strength and the ability to hold up the ball. He made ghostly runs between the lines, released team-mates with deft touches and made angled runs to bring others into play without even receiving the ball. A phantom goal-getter.

Raúl: the thinking man's forward

THE FINAL

REAL MADRID 1   0 JUVENTUS
Mijatovic 66

Date **20 May 1998** Stadium **Amsterdam Arena, Amsterdam**
Attendance **50,000** Referee **Helmut Krug (Germany)**

Marcello Lippi, one of Juventus's greatest managers, called it the dream final – and he was probably right, even if it turned into something of a nightmare for his team. Here were the giants of Italy taking on the self-appointed giants of Spain: but this was Juve's third successive appearance in a Champions League final (with victory coming in 1996), whereas Real Madrid had not won the competition in 32 years.

The stage was set then for a showpiece final and while it didn't turn out to be a cracker of Premier League proportions – lacking end-to-end drama and breakneck pace – it certainly entertained the deeper-thinking section of Europe's football support.

Initial pressure by Juventus was easily soaked up by a nervy *Los Blancos*, but, in the second half, Real Madrid began to assert themselves more, culminating in the game's 66th-minute goal. A deflected shot from the left by Roberto Carlos was picked up in the box by the tricky Yugoslav Predrag Mijatovic, who neatly sidestepped Angelo Peruzzi before clipping the ball into the net.

Real Madrid's team in the final consisted of players from eight nations: Spain, Germany, Argentina, Italy, Brazil, France, Holland and Yugoslavia. The club's tradition of buying the best to be the best, established during their most successful era between 1955 and 1960, was re-emerging to great effect.

Bizarrely, two days after winning the final, Jupp Heynckes was sacked as Real Madrid coach because of a lack of success in the Spanish domestic league.

THE LINE-UPS

Illgner, Sanchis, Panucci, Roberto Carlos, Raúl (Amavisca 90), Hierro (c), Karembeu, Seedorf, Redondo, Mijatovic (Suker 89), Morientes (Jaime 82)

Peruzzi (c), Torricelli, Montero, Iuliano, Di Livio (Tacchinardi 45), Deschamps (Conte 78), Davids, Possetto (Fonseca 71), Zidane, Del Piero, Inzaghi

1998/99

Manchester United win their first Champions League trophy – the first side to do so having not won their domestic league the season before

▼ DID YOU KNOW?

■ Holders Real Madrid crashed out in the quarter-finals to an Andriy Shevchenko-inspired Dynamo Kyiv. He scored in the 1-1 draw in Spain and got both goals in the Ukrainian side's 2-0 home win. But a string of saves by Bayern's Oliver Kahn denied Valery Lobanovsky's stars a place in Europe's biggest match.

■ The final was played on what would have been Sir Matt Busby's 90th birthday.

Busby: United's true working-class hero

▼ TOP GOALSCORERS

Andriy Shevchenko, D Kyiv	8
Dwight Yorke, Man United	8
Zlatko Zahovic, Porto	7
Filippo Inzaghi, Juventus	6
Ruud van Nistelrooy, PSV	5
Nuno Gomes, Benfica	5

▼ ALSO IN 1998/99

■ **Ballon d'Or** Rivaldo (Barcelona)

■ **Mercury Music Prize** Gomez – Bring It On

■ **BBC Sports Personality of the Year** Michael Owen

■ **Oscar for best film** Shakespeare in Love

There's a maxim in the English Premier League that you should never write off Manchester United, no matter what the circumstances and certainly not because there is only a few minutes left on the clock. The 1998/99 Champions League final proved to be the perfect example of why.

This tournament was far from plain sailing for Alex Ferguson's men, though. They had lost their Premier League title to the free-flowing Arsenal side created by Arsène Wenger–the first manager from outside the British Isles to win the English top flight – and, therefore, had to begin their Champions League campaign in the preliminary knockout phase. They got a favourable draw and predictably, if efficiently, dispatched Polish champions LKS Lodz 2-0 on aggregate, to join other big qualifiers – Inter Milan, Bayern Munich, Galatasaray and Benfica – in the 24-club group stage.

UEFA were relieved to see such big guns reaching the group phase. A Milanese mob of advertising and sponsorship gurus – backed by Italy's former prime minister Silvio Berlusconi – had put together a proposal for a breakaway midweek European Superleague, with no promotion or relegation, just a guaranteed annual payday for the continent's biggest clubs. Matches would be screened worldwide on a pay-per-view basis.

But the 12 clubs (Ajax, Barcelona, Bayern Munich, Borussia Dortmund, Inter, Juventus, Liverpool, Manchester United, Marseille, Milan, Porto and Real Madrid) who had had their interest sparked by such grandiose pledges of wealth were content to stay in UEFA's

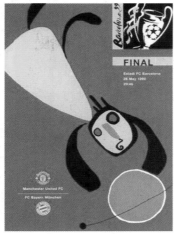

comfortable bed so long as their slice of the pie got a bit thicker. Increased match fees and points bonuses escalated the competition's rewards: Real Madrid earned £8m by winning the trophy in 1998, but nearly double that amount four years later.

Manchester United reached the knockout phase, but finished as best runners-up behind Bayern Munich, with whom they had drawn twice. In the quarter-finals, they gained a 2-0 advantage over Inter at Old Trafford, which the Italian side could not overturn in Milan.

Ferguson's men appeared to be on their way out at the semi-final stage, after drawing 1-1 at home to Juventus, Ryan Giggs scoring their injury-time equaliser. They then went 2-0 down within 11 minutes of the second leg thanks to two typically clinical Filippo Inzaghi strikes. However, United not only scored in Turin – a feat in itself – but won 2-3, a late goal from Dwight Yorke setting up a meeting with Bayern Munich in the final. Oh, the gall of it!

United won the title in the very last seconds of one of the most exciting finals ever – and made perhaps the unlikeliest comeback in history

THE FINAL

MAN UNITED 2   1 BAYERN MUNICH

Sheringham 90+1,   Basler 6
Solskjaer 90+3

Date **26 May 1999** Stadium **Camp Nou, Barcelona**
Attendance **90,000** Referee **Pierluigi Collina (Italy)**

And so to one of the most memorable European finals ever. The teams had twice crossed swords in the group stages and drawn both times, but this third encounter had fireworks aplenty.

Two yellow cards in the knockout phase meant United's inspirational captain Roy Keane couldn't take part in the final and the Red Devils missed their Irish talisman, conceding possession early on and a free-kick just outside their own area. Goalkeeper Peter Schmeichel, playing his last match for the club, set up the wall, but Mario Basler found a gap and the far corner – 1-0.

Bayern continued to exert their authority, intermittently running United ragged and twice hitting the post, but Alex Ferguson's men refused to lie down. In the 90th minute, after a defensive kerfuffle caused by Schmeichel's presence in the Bayern penalty area for a David Beckham corner, Ryan Giggs' weak shot was diverted into the goal by substitute Teddy Sheringham for the equaliser. The United players started to believe.

Two minutes later, with Bayern in disarray, a second United substitute – the 'Baby-faced Assassin' Ole Gunnar Solskjaer – won another corner kick. He then got on the end of Sheringham's near-post glance to score.

Manchester United had won the title in the very last seconds of one of the most exciting finals ever – and made possibly *the* unlikeliest comebacks in the history of sport. And they hadn't lost a single game en route to lifting their first Champions League trophy.

THE LINE-UPS

V

Schmeichel (c), G Neville, Irwin, Johnsen, Stam, Beckham, Butt, Blomqvist (Sheringham 67), Giggs, Cole (Solskjaer 81), Yorke

Kahn (c), Babbel, Kuffour, Matthäus (Fink 80), Linke, Tarnat, Jeremies, Effenberg, Basler (Salihamidzic 90), Zickler (Scholl 71), Jancker

1999/00

**Steve McManaman becomes the first English player to win the trophy
with a foreign club, in a tournament dominated by Spanish sides**

▼ DID YOU KNOW?

■ In Holland and Belgium 2000, France became the first country to win a European Championship straight after a World Cup. Their talisman, Zinedine Zidane, would not win the CL until moving to Real Madrid in 2001.
■ The last Cup Winner's Cup final at Villa Park and won by Lazio, 2-1 against Real Mallorca. No club ever retained the trophy – this was known as the 'CWC jinx'.

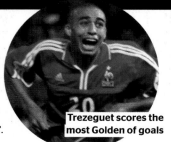

**Trezeguet scores the
most Golden of goals**

▼ TOP GOALSCORERS

Mário Jardel, Porto	10
Raúl González, Real Madrid	10
Rivaldo, Barcelona	10
Simone Inzaghi, Lazio	9
Serhiy Rebrov, Dynamo Kyiv	9
Tore Andre Flo, Chelsea	8
Patrick Kluivert, Barcelona	7
Paulo Sérgio, Bayern Munich	7

▼ ALSO IN 1999/00

■ **Ballon d'Or**
Luís Figo
(Real Madrid)
■ **Mercury Music Prize** Talvin Singh – OK
■ **BBC Sports Personality of the Year** Lennox Lewis
■ **Oscar for best film** American Beauty

The new millennium brought a whole set of changes to the Champions League, which – for the first time – would result in a final contested by two clubs from the same country (neither of whom were champions of Spain). This season also ushered in a new era of football wealth, the extent of which could not previously have been imagined.

But let's start with the format: 1999/2000 brought about a dramatic expansion of the competition. There would now be two qualifying rounds – the first with eight groups of four battling to qualify for a second group phase of 16 teams, who would fight it out to reach the quarter-final stage. More games, more goals to be had, more records to be broken and much more money to be made.

Teams who finished third in the first group phase would be entered into the latter stages of the revamped UEFA Cup, which would also feature all European domestic cup winners now that the Cup Winners' Cup was no more.

French champions Olympique Lyonnais were embarrassingly and comprehensively eliminated 3-0 in the third qualifying round by Maribor of Slovenia and Rangers – with only one Scotsman, Barry Ferguson, on the pitch – saw off UEFA Cup holders Parma at the same stage.

AC Milan also surprisingly exited the competition in the first group phase, coming bottom of a group containing Chelsea (first), Hertha BSC (second) and Galatasaray (third), the latter consoled by going on to win the UEFA Cup.

A revamped Barcelona were the only team to get through both group stages unbeaten. However,

despite smashing Chelsea 5-1 at the Nou Camp in the secong leg of the quarter-finals to win 6-4 on aggregate, their astonishing 4-1 semi-final first-leg defeat by Valencia in the Estadio Mestella was too much of a deficit to overcome. Barça could only win their home leg 2-1.

The holders, Manchester United, were bested 2-3 in their own backyard in a sensational quarter-final at Old Trafford, where Ronaldo scored a hat-trick and Fernando Redondo controlled proceedings despite the presence of Roy Keane and Paul Scholes in United's line-up. Alongside ex-Liverpool schemer McManaman, the Argentinian not only undid United, but also sparked the interest of a certain Russian oligarch in football (see page 4).

Nicolas Anelka, previously at odds with coach Vicente del Bosque, made up with his manager and scored home and away in the semi-final against Bayern Munich to secure a second final in three years for *Los Blancos*.

Alongside former Liverpool schemer McManaman, Redondo undid Valencia *and* sparked Roman Abramovioch's interest in football

(see page 4)

▼ PLAYER OF THE TOURNAMENT

■ **Fernando Redondo, Real Madrid**
The forgotten man of Real Madrid's wonderful midfield, the Argentinian would pick and prod at an opposition until they gradually unfurled. Good in the tackle, a great reader of play and with immensely quick feet, Redondo had everything – and he showed it to full effect during Real Madrid's 3-2 quarter-final victory at Old Trafford.

Redondo – UEFA's Club Footballer of 1999/2000

THE FINAL

REAL MADRID 3   0 VALENCIA

Morientes 39,
McManaman 67, Raúl 75

Date **24 May 2000** Stadium **Stade de France, Paris**
Attendance **78,759** Referee **Stefano Braschi (Italy)**

To football fans outside of Spain, Valencia were very much the surprise package of the 1999/2000 campaign. But with a rampant Gaizka Mendieta pulling the strings, and on-form Claudio Lopez and Kily Gonzalez immensely dangerous in the final third of the pitch, they were certainly not to be sniffed at – as Lazio and Barcelona found out in the knockout stages. But it wasn't to be for *Los Che* in the final.

Madrid stalwart Fernando Morientes, only playing because of an injury to the Brazilian Savio, headed home Michel Salgado's cross after 39 minutes and Valencia's inability to score from several chances before half-time would cost them dear.

A ruthless, quickfire double from Madrid ended the match as a contest in the second half. After 67 minutes, former Liverpool playmaker Steve McManaman spectacularly volleyed a half-cleared Roberto Carlos throw-in into the net – vindicating his much-derided departure from the Reds – and, five minutes later, ghostly frontman Raúl cleverly took the ball around Valencia keeper Santiago Canizares to slot home the third. Game over – and Manuel Sanchís, the 35-year-old club captain, was brought on in the final minutes to lift the trophy.

It was the first time since the advent of the European Cup/Champions League in 1955 that two clubs from the same country had competed in the final, but the tournament was receiving more attention than ever from all corners of the continent.

THE LINE-UPS

Casillas, Salgado (Hierro 85), Campo, Karanka, Roberto Carlos, Raúl (c), Redondo, Helguera, McManaman, Anelka (Sanchís 80), Morientes (Savio 72)

Canizares, Angloma, Pellegrino, Dukic, Gerardo (Ilie 69), Mendieta (c), Farinos, Gerard, Kily Gonzalez, Angulo, Claudio Lopez

2000/01

Valencia pay the penalty when the final turns into a battle of nerve, but a certain Yorkshire outfit suffer more for their dreamy over-extension

▼ DID YOU KNOW?

■ Juventus failed so miserably they even missed a spot in the UEFA Cup.
■ Deportivo La Coruna qualified for the tournament as champions of Spain, the smallest city (population roughly 200,000) to have won La Liga.
■ 2001 represented Bayern's fourth win in eight European Cup finals: a decent 50% yield. They would be unlucky to lower that figure in 2012 against Chelsea.

Mauro Silva: Depor's midfield rock

▼ TOP GOALSCORERS

Raúl González, Real Madrid	7
Elber, Bayern Munich	6
Iván Helguera, Real Madrid	6
Mário Jardel, Galatasaray	6
Rivaldo, Barcelona	6
Paul Scholes, Man United	6
Marco Simone, AS Monaco	6

▼ ALSO IN 2000/01

■ **Ballon d'Or** Michael Owen (Liverpool)
■ **Mercury Music Prize** Badly Drawn Boy – The Hour Of the Bewilderbeast
■ **BBC Sports Personality of the Year** Steve Redgrave
■ **Oscar for best film** Gladiator

Despite Valencia heroically battling their way to another Champions League final, in the San Siro against Bayern Munich, most of the talk in Spain was about the outrageous *Galactico* policy of new Real Madrid owner and property magnate, Florentino Pérez.

His first acquisition was a bold and highly controversial one: that of Barcelona's Luís Figo. The Portuguese winger became one of very few players ever to have transferred between the fierce rivals and the move was met with such fury on his return to the Camp Nou that Figo had missiles thrown at him, including a pig's head.

Another club in white who were 'living the dream', according to their chairman Peter Ridsdale, was Leeds United. Besuited types behind the scenes had recognised the vast wealth on offer courtesy of Europe's foremost club competition and invested robustly – some would say foolishly – in a talented crop of new players. However, loans were taken out against future Champions League income and, despite losing this season to Valencia in the semi-finals, Leeds missed out on qualification in 2001. So began their financial implosion and ignominious journey down to English football's third tier.

Meanwhile, Spartak Moscow pushed Bayer Leverkusen further down football's pecking order, ousting them from Group A; Sturm Graz of Austria surprisingly topped a group containing Rangers, Galatasaray and Monaco; and Juventus bowed out of the competition early again thanks to an embarrassing 1-3 home defeat by Hamburg and another 3-1 reverse,

away to Panathinaikos in their ultimate Group E match.

Amid claims of racist abuse of their black players at the Estadio Mestella, Arsenal lost on away goals to eventual finalists Valencia in the last eight. Manchester United also exited the tournament at this stage, Bayern Munich beating Ferguson's men 0-1 at Old Trafford and 2-1 in the Olympiastadion. For the second time in successive years, England's premier team had gone out to the eventual Champions League winners.

For a team once considered a Spanish yo-yo side, Deportivo La Coruna gave an astonishing account of themselves, reaching the quarter-finals before losing 2-3 to Leeds. New *Galactico* Figo scored an away goal for Real Madrid in the second leg of their semi-final against Bayern Munich, but *Los Blancos* still lost 3-1 on aggregate.

In the other semi-final, Valencia earned a battling 0-0 at Elland Road and then took apart Ridsdale's upstarts 3-0 in the return leg.

Once considered a Spanish yo-yo side, Deportivo La Coruna gave an astonishing account of themselves, reaching the quarter-finals

THE FINAL

BAYERN MUNICH 1   1 VALENCIA

Effenberg 50 (pen)   Mendieta 3 (pen)
AET Bayern Munich won 5-4 on penalties

Date **23 May 2001** Stadium **San Siro, Milan**
Attendance **70,000** Referee **Dick Jol (Holland)**

They were making history for the football-mad inhabitants of Spain's third-largest city (behind Madrid and Barcelona), but there was one thing Valencia did not want to achieve for posterity. Yes, they had reached another Champions League final, but, no, they did not want to become the first club to lose two finals in a row.

It didn't look as if they would after three minutes, when Bayern's Swedish defender Patrik Andersson handled the ball in his own penalty area and Valencia's coveted captain and playmaker, Gaizka Mendieta, assuredly converted the resulting spot-kick.

Four minutes later, *Die Bayern* had a penalty of their own after Stefan Effenberg was tripped, but Mehmet Scholl's spot-kick was dramatically diverted on to the

crossbar off the legs of Valencia keeper Santiago Canizares.

In the 50th minute, it became obvious this final was going to be a game of nerve and spot-kicks as yet another one was awarded to Bayern. Effenberg, wearing the captain's armband, took charge this time and made no mistake to draw his side level.

Fast-forward 70 minutes and the destination of the trophy would be decided by more of the dreaded 12-yard kicks.

To cut a long story a bit shorter, Bayern Munich's redoubtable goalkeeper Oliver Kahn – nicknamed *Der Titan* – saved three Valencia penalties in the shootout to help his side lift the Champions League trophy for the first time since 1975/76. Germans and penalties, eh?

THE LINE-UPS

Kahn, Sagnol (Jancker 46), Kuffour, Andersson, Lizarazu, Scholl (Sergio 108), Effenberg (c), Hargreaves, Linke, Salihamidzic, Elber (Zickler 100)

Canizares, Angloma, Ayala (Dukic 90), Pellegrino, Carboni, Mendieta (c), Sanchez (Zahovic 66), Aimar (Albelda 46), Baraja, Kily Gonzalez, Carew

2001/02

Duscher enjoyed a tackle, Beckham enjoyed another summer to forget and Madrid enjoyed a centenary celebration to remember

▼ DID YOU KNOW?

■ Manchester United's David Beckham missed the semi-final against Leverkusen, and had a below-par 2002 World Cup, thanks to Deportivo's Aldo Duscher, who broke the midfielder's metatarsal during a tackle in the quarter-final.
■ In 2001/02, Bayer Leverkusen achieved a treble of sorts: they finished as runners-up in the Bundesliga, the German cup and the Champions League.

Duscher: the bane of Old Trafford and Blighty

▼ TOP GOALSCORERS

Ruud van Nistelrooy, Man U	10
David Trezeguet, Juventus	8
Ole Gunnar Solskjaer, Man U	7
Thierry Henry, Arsenal	7

▼ ALSO IN 2001/02

■ **Ballon d'Or** Ronaldo (Real Madrid)
■ **Mercury Music Prize** PJ Harvey – Stories From The City, Stories From The Sea
■ **BBC Sports Personality of the Year** David Beckham
■ **Oscar for best film** Gladiator

It was to be the end of an era at Old Trafford. Sir Alex Ferguson – the man responsible for reversing Manchester United's ailing fortunes – had announced his impending retirement from the touchline, perhaps for a cosier position 'upstairs'. Anyway, with the Champions League final due to be played at Hampden Park, in the Scotsman's home city of Glasgow, it almost seemed fated that United would pay tribute to their greatest manager by winning it. However, it wasn't to be.

Despite the free-scoring exploits of new signing Ruud van Nistelrooy – the Dutchman feeding voraciously off the generous wing work of David Beckham and Ryan Giggs – United would lose on away goals to unfashionable, Michael Ballack-led Bayer Leverkusen in the semi-finals. By February, Ferguson had agreed to stay in charge for another three years, but this wasn't enough to spur his Manchester troops on to Glasgow. No fairytale this time, Alex.

Away from Old Trafford, the world mourned the tragic events of 9/11, which coincided with the first games of the first group phase. Some coaches revealed later it was hard to motivate their players after they had witnessed such horror, but subsequent appeals to UEFA against results fell on deaf ears.

Real Madrid, now deep into Florentino Pérez's *Galactico* era after signing Zinedine Zidane from Juventus for an incredible 150 billion Italian lira (about £50m), were the first team to reach the second group stage, qualifying with two games to go.

A lacklustre Dynamo Kyiv – by now missing star man Andriy Shevchenko, who was busy tormenting defences

in the black and red of AC Milan – crashed out with just one win, while a toothless Lazio side finished behind Nantes, Galatasaray and PSV Eindhoven in Group D.

Arsenal were unlucky to be sunk in the next group phase. Under new rules, if points were level, group position was to be decided on head-to-head results rather than goal difference. Deportivo, having beaten the Gunners twice, knew they couldn't be beaten into second place by Arsenal, so put out a weakened side in their last match at home to Leverkusen, a team Arsenal had beaten 4-1 at Highbury. Deportivo lost 3-1, Leverkusen finished top, and Arsenal crashed out with Juventus.

In the game of the knockout round, dubbed the 'tie of the century' by the Spanish press, Steve McManaman and Zidane gave Real Madrid their first victory over Barcelona in Camp Nou in more than 20 years. A 1-1 draw in the return leg was enough to secure a third final in five years for *Los Blancos*.

Despite thrashing eventual finalists Bayer Leverkusen 4-1 at Highbury, Arsenal crashed out because of UEFA's new head-to-head rule

▼ PLAYER OF THE TOURNAMENT

■ **Zinedine Zidane, Real Madrid**
The greatest midfielder of his generation played in two finals for Juventus, but each time was on the losing side. However, his guile, tenacity and sheer class helped elevate a Real Madrid team of already gifted sportsmen – and Zidane won his first and only Champions League medal in his first full season at the club.

Zidane – a cut above the midfield pack

THE FINAL

REAL MADRID 2   1 B LEVERKUSEN

Raúl 9,   Lucio 14
Zidane 45

**Date 15 May 2002 Stadium Hampden Park, Glasgow
Attendance 52,000 Referee Urs Meier (Switzerland)**

Real Madrid's young goalkeeper, Móstoles-born Iker Casillas, made as significant a contribution to this Champions League final as their midfield talisman Zinedine Zidane, with his fluid orchestration of play and exquisitely executed 45th-minute goal.

Casillas was called into action as *Los Blancos*, 2-1 up, were coming under mounting pressure from Michael Ballack's stubborn Bayer Leverkusen. He replaced the experienced, but injured, César Sánchez with barely 20 minutes left to play and, deep into injury time, the 20-year-old proved his increasing worth, pulling off three spectacular saves to deny the Germans an equaliser.

Despite referee Urs Meier signaling seven minutes of overtime and Leverkusen – in a bid to become the fourth German name on the trophy – pushing forward with all their teutonic might, it was not to be.

In their centenary year, Real Madrid wrote another wonderful chapter in their history at Hampden Park: the Glasgow stadium also being the venue for their systematic 7-3 destruction of another German side, Eintracht Frankfurt, in the 1960 final.

The 2002 final proved a lot different, though. Real were pegged back almost immediately by a vicious Lucio header after 14 minutes, but regained the lead through a wondrous strike by Zidane just before half-time and then desperately held on for victory. But the result was no less significant. Could Barcelona ever compete with their might?

THE LINE-UPS

César (Casillas 68), Salgado, Hierro (c), Helguera, Roberto Carlos, Figo (McManaman 61), Makelele (Conceicao 73), Zidane, Solari, Raúl, Morientes

Butt, Zivkovic, Lucio (Babic 90), Placente, Schneider, Sebescen (Kirsten 65), Ramelow (c), Ballack, Neuville, Basturk, Brdaric (Berbatov 38)

Legends

Scary goalkeepers, magical midfielders and sublime strikers: the ever-changing cast of the Champions League never fails to entertain

Ronaldo

Clubs: PSV Eindhoven, Barcelona, Internazionale, Real Madrid, Milan

Winner: N/A

Born: 18/09/76

At his peak, *Il Fenomeno* was an unstoppable force: powerful and pacy, with the ability to bend and break defences with rhythmic or staccato dribbles. A true wonder who became the toast of European football, he won the Ballon d'Or in 1997 and 2002, was runner-up in 1996 and third in 1998. He also won the FIFA World Player of the Year in 1996, 1997 and 2002.

Did you know?

Ronaldo never won the Champions League, but scored a hat-trick for Real Madrid at Old Trafford in 2003 – effectively knocking out Manchester United – and was applauded by both sets of supporters when exiting the field.

20

19

Thierry Henry

Clubs: Arsenal, Barcelona
Winner: 2008/09
Born: 17/08/77

At the peak of his powers, the Frenchman could glide past defenders as if they weren't there. He spent his final two seasons at Arsenal as captain and literally led from the front, scoring the goals that took the Gunners to the Champions League final in 2006, when they were beaten 2-1 by Barcelona. Henry finally got his hands on the trophy as a Barça player during the Spanish club's sextuple-winning season of 2008/09, beating Manchester United 2-0 in the final.

Did you know?
Henry was runner-up in the 2003 and 2004 FIFA World Player of the Year awards.

18

David Beckham

Clubs: Manchester United, Real Madrid
Winner: 1998/99
Born: 02/05/75

Beckham was the world's highest-paid footballer in 2004, with wages and endorsements, but he only lifted one Champions League title, with his beloved Manchester United in their treble-winning season of 1998/99. It was a special year for 'Goldenballs', who also picked up the UEFA Club Midfielder of the Year and UEFA Club Footballer of the Year awards.

Did you know?
Beckham was the first England player to collect two red cards – against Argentina in 1998 and Austria in 2005, when he also became the first England captain to be sent off.

17

Iker Casillas

Clubs: Real Madrid
Winner: 1999/00, 2001/02
Born: 20/05/81

Spain's most successful captain – having led them to two European Championship (2008 and 2012) and one World Cup (2010) victory – Casillas is one of the world's best keepers, famed for his shot stopping and an almost telepathic ability in one-on-one situations. His reactions and his record have earned him numerous awards including Best European Goalkeeper in 2008 and 2010, and he has twice lifted the Champions League trophy with Real Madrid, in 1999/00 and 2001/02.

Did you know?
Casillas holds the world record for the most international clean sheets with 73.

16

Alessandro Del Piero

Clubs: Juventus
Winner: 1995/96
Born: 09/09/74

The all-time record goalscorer, with 289, at 'The Old Lady' of Italian football, Del Piero is as synonymous with Juventus as the black-and-white striped shirts. He helped the *Bianconeri* win the Champions League trophy in 1996, when they beat Ajax on penalties in the final, and was a runner-up in 1997, 1998 and 2003.

Did you know?
Del Piero is famed for scoring from a particular part of the pitch (coming in from the left wing and curling the ball into the top, right-hand corner), a phenomenon Juventus fans have dubbed *Gol alla Del Piero*.

15

Javier Zanetti

Clubs: Internazionale
Winner: 2009/10
Born: 10/08/73

An Inter Milan stalwart since 1995, during which time he has picked up the moniker *El Tractor* for his bulldozing resilience on the pitch, Zanetti didn't realise his dream of lifting the Champions League trophy until 2009/10, at which time he became the first player to captain an Italian team to the Scudetto, Coppa Italia and Champions League treble.

Did you know?
Zanetti's appearance for Internazionale in the 2009/10 Champions League final, in which they beat Bayern Munich 2-0, was his 700th for the club.

14

Paul Scholes

Clubs: Manchester United
Winner: 1998/99, 2007/08
Born: 16/11/74

Another one-club legend, having played for Manchester United for the whole of his career. Scholes picked up a yellow card in the 1999 Champions League semi-final against Juventus, which ruled him out of the club's dramatic 2-1 final victory over Bayern Munich. He was also substituted before the 2008 penalty shootout, but remains a Champions League legend nonetheless and is among the tournament's top 10 appearance-makers.

Did you know?
Scholes holds the record for the most yellow cards in the Champions League, with 32.

13

A. Shevchenko

Clubs: Dynamo Kiev, Milan, Chelsea
Winner: 2002/03
Born: 29/09/76

The fifth-highest scorer in Champions League history – behind Thierry Henry, Lionel Messi, Ruud van Nistelrooy and Raúl (see pg8) – Shevchenko was the first Ukrainian-born player to lift the trophy when AC Milan beat Juventus on penalties in 2002/03. He is also the top scorer in the *Derby della Madonnina* (Milan derby). After the 2003 win, he flew to Kiev to lay his medal on the grave of footballing mastermind Valeri Lobanovsky, whom he played under at Dynamo Kyiv.

Did you know?
Shevchenko's family were forced out of their home in 1986 after the Chernobyl nuclear disaster.

12

Oliver Kahn

Clubs: Karlsruher SC, Bayern Munich
Winner: 2000/01
Born: 15/06/69

Der Titan is one of the most successful players in the history of German football and was a formidable, almost alarming, presence during his time between the sticks at Bayern Munich. This intimidating style came in use during Bayern's Champions League final penalty shootout victory over Valencia in 2001, as Kahn saved no less than three efforts from Zlatko Zahovic, Amedeo Carboni *and* Mauricio Pellegrini.

Did you know?
Kahn was name Best European Goalkeeper for four years running between 1999 and 2002.

11

Andrés Iniesta

Clubs: Barcelona
Winner: 2005/06, 2008/09, 2010/11
Born: 11/05/84

Named as Player of the Tournament at Euro 2012, Spain's Andrés Iniesta is an integral cog in Barcelona's short-passing machine. He is also a very versatile player, who can perform as an out-and-out winger, a central midfielder, a holding midfielder or a 'false' No9. Spain manager Vicente del Bosque described Iniesta as "the complete footballer. He can attack and defend, he creates and scores".

Did you know?
Iniesta's array of talents – as well as his less-than-bronzed skin – have earned him multiple nicknames including *El Ilusionista* (The Illusionist), *El Cerebro* (The Brain) and *El Caballero Pálido* (The Pale Knight).

10

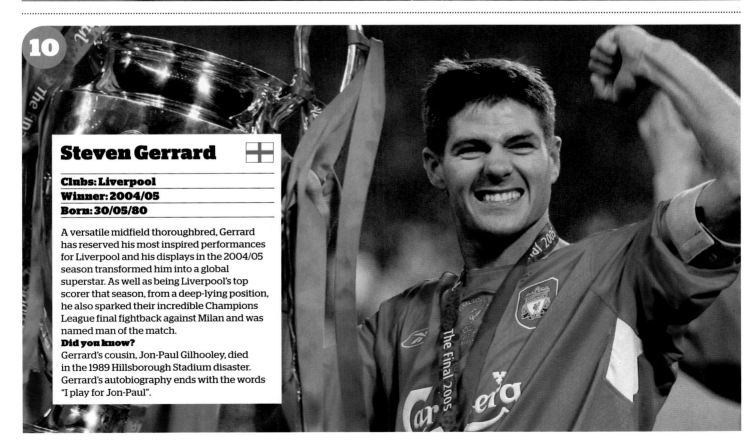

Steven Gerrard

Clubs: Liverpool
Winner: 2004/05
Born: 30/05/80

A versatile midfield thoroughbred, Gerrard has reserved his most inspired performances for Liverpool and his displays in the 2004/05 season transformed him into a global superstar. As well as being Liverpool's top scorer that season, from a deep-lying position, he also sparked their incredible Champions League final fightback against Milan and was named man of the match.

Did you know?
Gerrard's cousin, Jon-Paul Gilhooley, died in the 1989 Hillsborough Stadium disaster. Gerrard's autobiography ends with the words "I play for Jon-Paul".

Samuel Eto'o

Clubs: Real Madrid, Mallorca, Barcelona, Internazionale, Anzhi
Winner: 2005/06, 2008/09, 2009/10
Born: 10/03/81

One of the first African players to become a true superstar at a premier European club, Eto'o was only the second player, after Raúl, to score in two separate Champions League finals. He is also only the fourth player – behind Marcel Desailly, Paulo Sousa and Gerard Piqué – to have won the competition two years in succession with different club sides (Barça in 08/09 and Inter in 09/10).

Did you know?
Eto'o won the Champions League final man of the match award in 2006.

Luis Figo

Clubs: Sporting, Barcelona, Real Madrid, Internazionale
Winner: 2001/02
Born: 4/11/72

Portugal's most-capped player was also well decorated on the club circuit. A powerful dribbler and persistent assister, Figo is one of few players to have worn both the Barcelona and Real Madrid shirts (in that order). His defection to the Bernabéu signalled the start of the much-lauded *galactico* era and a Champions League victory in 2002 courtesy of that Zinedine Zidane volley.

Did you know?
Figo won four successive Serie A titles with Inter Milan before retiring in 2009.

Clarence Seedorf

Clubs: Ajax, Sampdoria, Real Madrid, Internazionale, Milan
Winner: 1994/95, 1997/98, 02/03, 06/07
Born: 1/04/76

The only player to have won the Champions League four times with three different clubs: Ajax in 1995, Real Madrid in 1998 and AC Milan in 2003 (on penalties against Juventus) and in 2007, when they gained revenge against Rafa Benítez's Liverpool. An incredible achievement for an athlete who added candour and gravity to the BBC's Euro 2012 punditry.

Did you know?
In 2011, Seedorf was awarded the Order of Orange-Nassau, comparable to an OBE, for charity work.

Ryan Giggs

Clubs: Manchester United
Winner: 1998/99, 2007/08
Born: 29/11/73

A wonderful Old Trafford servant who helped turn Sir Alex Ferguson's Manchester United into perennial Premier League champions. In 1996/97, Giggs helped United to reach the Champions League semi-finals for the first time in 28 years. Two years later, he booked their passage to the final at Camp Nou, against Bayern Munich, with a 90th-minute equaliser against Juventus at Old Trafford. He also set up Teddy Sheringham's equaliser in the 1999 final and is the oldest scorer in Champions League history having hit the net against Benfica in September 2011 aged 37 years 289 days.

Did you know?
Giggs is the highest British scorer in European Cup history and has scored in 16 Champions League tournaments (11 consecutively).

Raúl

Clubs: Real Madrid, Schalke 04
Winner: 1997/98, 1999/00, 2001/02
Born: 27/06/77

Raúl never won anything significant with the Spanish national team, but certainly made an impression on Europe's premier club competition with Real Madrid. He is the all-time Champions League appearance-maker (144) and goalscorer (71), and was the first player to score in two Champions League finals – the 2000 all-Spanish affair against Valencia in the Stade de France and the 2002 contest against Bayer Leverkusen at Hampden Park, both of which Madrid won. They also lifted the trophy in 1998. Raúl was the first player to score 50 Champions League goals and, in the twilight of his career, he helped Schalke to their first Champions League semi-final in 2010/11. A truly glittering career.

Did you know?
Raúl was top scorer in the Champions League in 1999/00 and 2000/01, and was voted the tournament's Best Forward in the same years, and again in 2001/02.

5

Xavi

Clubs: Barcelona
Winner: 2005/06, 2008/09, 2010/11
Born: 25/01/80

An integral part of the sextuple-winning Barcelona side of 2009, Xavi has spent his entire career with the Catalan club and is one of the foremost exponents of the tiki-taka style of football espoused by Barça's renowned La Masia academy. 'The Puppet Master' is adept at finding and exploiting space, averaging more completed passes than any other midfielder in Europe. Reliable, ruthless and brilliantly reactive, Xavi is the most revered central midfielder on the planet.

Did you know?
Xavi has received five Ballon d'Or nominations and, in 2010, was named World Footballer of the Year.

4

Paolo Maldini

Clubs: Milan
Winner: 1993/94, 2002/03, 2006/07
Born: 26/06/68

In a footballing landscape tinged with greed and deceit, it's rare to witness a top player commit his whole career to one club: Paolo Maldini was such a man. Between 1985 and 2009 he played 902 times for AC Milan, earning the nickname *Il Capitano*, 'The Captain', and winning the European Cup in 1988/89 and 1989/90, and the Champions League in 1993/94, 2002/03 and 2006/07. He was voted man of the match in the 2002/03 final and held the record for the most European Cup and UEFA Champions League appearances, with 139, until this was equalled by Ryan Giggs and surpassed by Raúl (144).

Did you know?
Maldini holds the record for the most European Cup final appearances, eight, and he became the oldest player to have scored in a final when he netted after one minute against Liverpool in 2005, at the age of 36 years 333 days.

3

Lionel Messi

Clubs: Barcelona
Winner: 2005/06, 2008/09, 2010/11
Born: 24/06/87

Messi arrived at Barcelona with his family as a 13-year-old, ready to begin a course of hormone replacement for his growth deficiencies and the long journey to super-stardom. In 2012, he has most certainly arrived. 'Leo' is only the fourth footballer – alongside Johan Cruyff, Michel Platini and Marco van Basten – to win three Ballons d'Or, and only the second, after Platini to win three consecutive Ballons d'Or. He made Champions League history in 2012 by scoring five goals in the 7-1 victory over Bayer Leverkusen, the first player to score five times in one Champions League game.

Did you know?

Messi has scored the most goals in a single Champions League season, 14, and is the only player to have scored two hat-tricks in a Champions League season. He is also the only player to have earned the Top Scorer award four years in a row. Indisputably the world's most exhilarating footballing talent.

2

Zinedine Zidane

Clubs: Bordeaux, Juventus, Real Madrid

Winner: 2001/02

Born: 23/06/72

Despite being chased by Kenny Dalglish at Blackburn Rovers, Zidane joined Champions League winners Juventus in 1996/97 for a paltry £3.2m. They won Serie A in his first season, but Zidane failed to shake off the attentions of Paul Lambert in the Champions League final and Juventus lost 3-1 to Borussia Dortmund. 'Zizou' joined Real Madrid five years later for a whopping 150 billion Lira and scored *that* volley in the 2002 Champions League final against Bayer Leverkusen: his fourth appearance in European football's biggest match, but his first victory.

Did you know?

French defender Bixente Lizarazu once said of his national team-mate: "When we don't know what to do, we just give it to Zizou and he works something out." A unique conjuror who will never be replicated.

1

2002/03

A great year for Paolo Maldini, Serie A and Mediterranean hairdressers as Italian football makes a continental powerplay

▼ DID YOU KNOW?

■ David Beckham and Sir Alex Ferguson's relationship was at breaking point in 2002/03 culminating in the infamous 'boot-in-the-face' incident and a £25m move to Real Madrid materialising shortly afterwards.

■ Pavel Nedved, some pundits' player of the tournament, was magical against Real Madrid in the semi-final, but missed the final after one yellow card too many.

Pavel Nedved – because he's worth it!

▼ TOP GOALSCORERS

Ruud van Nistelrooy, Man Utd	12
Filippo Inzaghi, AC Milan	10
Roy Makaay, Deportivo	9
Hernán Crespo, Inter	9
Raúl González, Real Madrid	9
Jan Koller, Dortmund	8
Javier Saviola, Barcelona	7
Thierry Henry, Arsenal	7

▼ ALSO IN 2002/03

■ **Ballon d'Or**
Pavel Nedvěd
(Juventus)

■ **Mercury Music Prize**
A Little Deeper

■ **BBC Sports Personality of the Year** Paula Radcliffe

■ **Oscar for best film**
Chicago

A nother year of glory in black and red for Paolo Maldini. This time the perma-tanned stalwart lifted the trophy as captain after the *Rossoneri* won the first all-Italian final on penalty kicks.

It would be the last time the tournament would use two group stages, the second 4x4 team phase making way for a round-of-16 knockout phase in 2003/04.

The most embarrassing casualty of the first phase in 2002/03 were the mighty Bayern Munich. They did not win any of their six games in Group G, losing home and away to eventual group winners Milan and Deportivo La Coruna, and twice drawing with Lens.

Liverpool also crashed out. After a careless 1-0 defeat at home to Valencia, they could only draw 3-3 in their must-win final match against Christian Gross's battling Basel side and finished behind the Swiss champions, in third place.

Arsenal and Borussia Dortmund, despite having their difficulties, qualified with a game in hand from Group A – and, in a triumph for a rejuvenated Serie A, all four Italian clubs qualified for the next phase, with only Roma not topping their group. They finished second on goal difference to Real Madrid.

Predictably, then, only Roma failed at the next hurdle, bottoming out a group containing Valencia, Ajax and Arsenal. The big news of the second group stage was the sacking of Bayer Leverkusen's manager Klaus Toppmöller. A year earlier, he had been the toast of the city after leading his troops to a hard-fought final defeat by Real Madrid. But six losses in six group games brought about his demise.

Barcelona had been the only team to win all six of their games in the first group stage, albeit with a favourable draw against Lokomotiv Moscow, Club Brugge and Galatasaray. They remained undefeated in the second group phase, but lost 3-2 on aggregate to Juventus in the quarter-finals.

Juventus saved their best defensive football for the business end of the tournament, squeezing through Group D behind Manchester United and knocking out holders Real Madrid in the semi-finals, 4-3 on aggregate.

Madrid had beaten Manchester United in style in the quarter-finals, Ronaldo scoring a hat-trick at Old Trafford, but, crucially, *Los Blancos* were without Raúl in the semi-finals because the striker had appendicitis.

Inter were the third Italian club in the semi-finals, but lost on away goals to their city rivals, despite both sides playing their home matches at the San Siro. Andriy Shevchenko scored the crucial goal in first-half stoppage time in the return leg.

The big news of the first group phase was the sacking of Bayer Leverkusen's Klaus Toppmöller, who a year earlier had led his troops to the final

Harder to get past than a charity mugger

THE FINAL

AC MILAN 0   0 JUVENTUS

AET Milan won 4-2 on penalties

Date 28 May 2003 Stadium Old Trafford, Manchester
Attendance 63,215 Referee Markus Merk (Germany)

The 2002/03 Champions League denouement, between steadfast, experienced finalists, came down to pure bottle – and AC Milan simply had more of it.

The *Rossoneri* also had all of their best players available and chomping at the bit for selection, whereas Juventus's hugely influential playmaker, Pavel Nedved, was suspended – a bitter blow for the Old Lady's fans and neutrals alike.

The match missed the zip and vigour of the Czech schemer's work – and with Milan coach Carlo Ancelotti's intimate knowledge of Juventus (he managed them from 1999-2001), it was always likely to be a game of cat and mouse.

Few chances of note were created, but Milan used the ball so wisely that, even when Juventus effectively went a man up – Roque Junior buckling badly in injury time with no more substitutions available – they couldn't find the key to unlock a staunch, well-organised rearguard.

So the first all-Italian final idiosyncratically finished 0-0 after 120 minutes and had to be decided by penalties, a result that seemed to please both contestants.

David Trezeguet, Marcelo Zalayeta and Paolo Montero all missed for Juve, while Kakha Kaladze and Clarence Seedorf were off target for Milan. But after Andriy Shevchenko hit the winner past Juventus goalkeeper Gianluigi Buffon, we suspect this was swiftly forgotten amid the celebrations and realisation that Seedorf had become the first player to win the Champions League trophy with three clubs: Ajax (1995), Real Madrid (1998) and, now, AC Milan.

THE LINE-UPS

Dida, Nesta, Costacurta (Roque Junior 66), Maldini (c), Kaladze, Gattuso, Pirlo (Serginho 71), Rui Costa (Ambrosini 87), Seedorf, Shevchenko, Inzaghi

Buffon, Thuram, Ferrara, Montero, Tudor (Birindelli 42), Camoranesi (Conte 46), Tacchinardi, Davids (Zalayeta 65), Zambrotta, Del Piero (c), Trezeguet

2003/04

Monaco prove taxing, a jigging José Mourinho shows his worth at Porto and a ridiculously rich Russian begins a west London dynasty

▼ DID YOU KNOW?

■ Roman Abramovich was orphaned at a young age and grew up with his uncle. He launched his business career by selling plastic toy ducks from a Moscow flat and then moved into oil.

■ The principality of Monaco has lower tax rates than the rest of France, so players on big wages and with bigger reputations can be lured to play for them: the rest of France don't like this!

From small ducklings powerful oligarchs grow

▼ TOP GOALSCORERS

Fernando Morientes, Monaco	9
Dado Prso, Monaco	7
Roy Makaay, Bayern Munich	6
Walter Pandiani, Deportivo	6
Didier Drogba, Marseille	5
Hakan Sukur, Galatasaray	5
Juninho, Lyon	5
Thierry Henry, Arsenal	5

▼ ALSO IN 2003/04

■ **Ballon d'Or**
Andriy Shevchenko
(AC Milan)

■ **Mercury Music Prize** Boy In Da Corner

■ **BBC Sports Personality of the Year** Jonny Wilkinson

■ **Oscar for best film**
TLOTR: Return Of The King

The 2003/04 Champions League campaign was all about the underdog and the oligarch. Both had a profound effect on the game during this campaign, but one's influence would reverberate around the footballing landscape, changing it forever.

First we had the stunning over-achievements of José Mourinho's FC Porto. Then we had the over-exuberances of Roman Abramovich and the onset of his Russian revolution in the English Premier League: out went Chelsea and in came Chelski, the most extravagant club in the world.

It's thought the fabulously wealthy businessman fell in love with football, and primarily the Champions League, during the previous season, after seeing Real Madrid and Manchester United's quarter-final epic at Old Trafford. He bought Chelsea for £140m, instantly wiped out the club's debts as if paying off his milk bill, and hurriedly spent another £210m on the world's best footballing talent, including Argentina's Hernán Crespo for £16.8m, Ireland's Damien Duff for £17m, from Blackburn, Claude Makelele, Geremi, Adrian Mutu, Glen Johnson, Wayne Bridge and Joe Cole.

Chief executive Peter Kenyon was also nabbed from Manchester United to control efforts off the pitch and Claudio Ranieri – the much-lauded and well-travelled 'Tinkerman' – would stay in the manager's hotseat until Abramovich deemed otherwise. He was very unlucky to lose his job in the end, having come second in the Premier League and reaching the semi-finals of the Champions League before being knocked out by a very decent Monaco side, 5-3 on aggregate.

The competition format had altered again. Because of some abject European displays in the 2002 World Cup, UEFA president Lennart Johansson insisted the second 4x4-team group stage should become a 16-team knockout phase. It didn't appeal to the 'big 14' at first – less games meant less revenue – but sense was seen and plans put in place.

Lyon topped Group A, which also contained Bayern Munich, while Arsenal – who only garnered one point from their first three matches – stormed into the knockout stage, winning 1-5 against Inter at the San Siro. Monaco were in fine fettle too, beating Deportivo La Coruna, who somehow also qualified, 8-3, and knocking out Real Madrid in their quarter-final after scoring two away goals in the Bernabéu, including one by Madrid loanee and tournament top scorer Fernando Morientes. Mourinho, meanwhile, did *that* jig down the Old Trafford touchline as his Porto side beat United in their own backyard.

Even before the game had begun, it was pretty common knowledge that the master tactician behind Porto's unlikely Champions League ascent was on his way to Chelsea. The Blues' new hands-on benefactor, Roman Abramovich, was promising José Mourinho unlimited funds with which to try to capture Europe's ultimate prize for him.

Porto had won the UEFA Cup in 2002/03 (beating Celtic 3-2 in Seville) and this experience made them favourites for the Champions League final in the bookie's eyes. But a stuttering first half did nothing to separate the teams until – against the run of play and despite Monaco captain Ludovic Giuly's scintillating form – Porto took the lead. Their Brazilian striker, Carlos Alberto, unselfishly laid off the ball, but it rebounded to him of a defender, so he decided to score instead.

Porto wrapped up the game in the second half after Mourinho's clever substitution. He brought on Dmitri Alenichev, who beat the Monaco offside trap twice in quick succession, first punishing the French team by setting up Deco's goal and then going through on his own to seal the deal. A one-sided scoreline after a fairly even match.

The Porto side broke up quickly after their European success – Ricardo Carvalho and Paulo Ferreira went with Mourinho to Chelsea, while Deco left for Barcelona – and their supreme underdog story would be usurped just one year later by some men in red from England's north-west.

Abramovich brought his Russian revolution to the Premier League: out went Chelsea, in came Chelski, the most extravagant club in the world

Vitor Baia (c), Paulo Ferreira, Carvalho, Costa, Valente, Costinha, Mendes, Deco (Emanuel 85), Maniche, Derlei (McCarthy 79), Carlos Alberto (Alenichev 60)

Roma, Ibarra, Rodriguez, Givet (Squillaci 72), Evra, Cissé (Nonda 64), Bernardi, Zikos, Rothen, Giuly (c, Prso 68), Morientes

▼ PLAYER OF THE TOURNAMENT

■ Deco, Porto

A diminutive, attacking midfielder, Deco is Brazilian by birth, but changed his nationality to Portuguese after settling so naturally into the country. His prodding and probing of Monaco's defence in the Champions League final – and his nonchalant, sidefooted goal – earned him the man of the match award.

Deco: reunited with José Mourinho at Chelsea

2004/05

A long European adventure began in the Austrian wilderness and ended in Istanbul, where the streets were painted a sea of Anfield red

▼ DID YOU KNOW?

■ Manchester United striker Ruud van Nistelrooy, bagging eight Champions League goals, was the tournament's top scorer for the third time in four seasons.
■ In the quarter-final, Liverpool faced Juventus for the first time since 33 Juve and six Reds fans died in the Heysel disaster of 1985. Some of Juventus' more fervent support turned their back (literally) on a remembrance gesture made by Liverpool fans at the start of the game.

Score? It would be Ruud not to

▼ TOP GOALSCORERS

Ruud van Nistelrooy Man Utd	8
Adriano Inter	7
Roy Makaay Bayern Munich	7
Sylvain Wiltord Lyon	6
Hernán Crespo AC Milan	6
Andriy Shevchenko AC Milan	6

▼ ALSO IN 2004/05

■ **Ballon d'Or** Ronaldinho (Barcelona)
■ **Mercury Music Prize** Franz Ferdinand
■ **BBC Sports Personality of the Year** Kelly Holmes
■ **Oscar for best film** Million Dollar Baby

Another gripping Champions League campaign culminated in the most exciting, most dramatic finale in the history of the competition – past, present and (to date) future. Fitting then, that at the centre of this perfect storm were Liverpool FC, the most decorated English club in European football and – because of a lack of recent success – a club that brings to mind a glorious, halcyon era.

The Reds' journey to the final began on 11 August 2004, against Austrian side Grazer AK in the Arnold Schwarzenegger Stadium, and featured a spectacular performance and two goals from Steven Gerrard. The Liverpool stalwart had refused to have his head turned by Roman Abramovich's billions in west London, despite firm and hugely lucrative offers apparently on the table.

But if Gerrard's time felt borrowed, Michael Owen's was almost over at Anfield. He sat on the bench for the Grazer AK match to ensure he wasn't cup-tied and was later transferred to Real Madrid for £8m.

The group stages provided little in the way of surprises: Abramovich's two footballing interests were paired together in Group H, CSKA Moscow succumbing to Chelsea, and also Porto, to crash out early. Lyon, now *the* team to beat in France, topped a group containing Manchester United, while Arsenal limped to four draws, but still topped Group E, with tournament dark horses PSV Eindhoven slotting in behind them.

Liverpool only just scraped through behind Monaco in Group A thanks to a long-range Gerrard piledriver, three minutes from the

end of their final group game against Greek outfit Olympiakos.

Chelsea squeezed past Barcelona in the first knockout round. Despite José Mourinho serving a touchline ban, they won 4-2 at Stamford Bridge, and 5-4 on aggregate, then beat Bayern Munich by the same score in the first leg of the quarter-final to set up an intriguing semi-final clash with Liverpool. The Blues had outgunned the Reds in the English League Cup final in February.

Liverpool, strangely, owed their 1-0 semi-final victory to Sepp Blatter's refusal to adopt goalline technology. A hugely controversial Luis García 'goal' – which pundits, after numerous replays, still couldn't establish was over the line – sent Liverpool through to Istanbul.

Their opponents would be Milan, who humiliated their city rivals, Inter, 5-0 on aggregate in the quarter-finals, after beating Manchester United in the round of 16. They then squeezed past PSV on away goals in their semi-final.

THE FINAL

LIVERPOOL 3   3 MILAN

Gerrard 53, Smicer 55, Alonso 59   Maldini 1, Crespo 38, 43
AET Liverpool won 3-2 on penalties

Date **25 May 2005** Stadium **Ataturk Stadium, Istanbul**
Attendance **69,000** Referee **Manuel Mejuto González (Spain)**

After only 53 seconds of the final, Andrea Pirlo's free-kick, conceded by Liverpool's perceived weak link, Djimi Traoré, was headed into the Reds' net by Milan captain Paolo Maldini. Rafael Benítez's gameplan was instantly undone by the *Rossoneri*.

Still evidently carrying an injury, Harry Kewell, a starting gamble, was replaced by Vladimir Smicer after 22 minutes, but to little effect. Inspirational playmaker Kaká was finding far too much room between the Liverpool lines and, 16 minutes after the substitution, he carved out Milan's second goal for Hernán Crespo. Five minutes later, Crespo repeated the feat and Milan went into the dressing room 3-0 up.

A combination of things spurred Liverpool's revival: Milan's apparent over-confidence at half-time, an injured Steve Finnan forcing Benítez into having a back three, and German stopper Dietmar Hamann being used to plug gaps in Liverpool's midfield.

Eight minutes into the second half, Liverpool captain Steven Gerrard started the comeback, heading in a pinpoint cross from John Arne Riise. Incredibly, six minutes later, they were level, Smicer scoring with a driven shot and Xavi Alonso converting a Gerrard-won penalty.

An hour later, neither goalline had been breached again, thanks mainly to the efforts of Reds keeper Jerzy Dudek, who then also saved Andriy Shevchenko's penalty in the shootout to win Liverpool the trophy. The greatest European final ever.

Liverpool scraped past Olympiakos and through the group thanks to a long-range Gerrard piledriver, three minutes from the final whistle

▼ **PLAYER OF THE TOURNAMENT**

■ **Steven Gerrard, Liverpool**
Liverpool captain, catalyst, engine room, playmaker and heart, Gerrard had the European season of his life in 2004/05. Look anywhere on this page and you'll see or read about him. He started superbly in Graz in August 2004 and his level did not drop until he was lifting the trophy in Istanbul. Inspirational stuff.

Dragged the Reds to Istanbul by their heels

THE LINE-UPS

Dudek, Finnan (Hamann 46), Carragher, Hyppia, Traoré, Luis García, Gerrard (c), Alonso, Riise, Baros (Cissé 85), Kewell (Smicer 22)

Dida, Cafu, Nesta, Stam, Maldini (c), Kaká, Pirlo, Gattuso (Rui Costa 112), Seedorf (Serginho 86), Crespo (Tomasson 85), Shevchenko

2005/06

Football purists are happy as the continent's two best passing teams meet in its most prestigious match. A cracker was on the cards...

WINNE
UEFA CHAMPIONS

▼ DID YOU KNOW?

■ Liverpool began the campaign to retain their Champions League trophy a mere 48 days after they had held it aloft in Istanbul.

■ In 2005, Malcolm Glazer bought out the shareholders in Manchester United, to the chagrin of some fans who branched off to create FC United. Since 2005, ticket prices at Old Trafford have increased by more than 40%.

"Could you be more clear, please?"

▼ TOP GOALSCORERS

Andriy Shevchenko AC Milan	9
Ronaldinho Barcelona	7
David Trezeguet Juventus	6
Samuel Eto'o Barcelona	6
Adriano Inter	5
Johan Micoud Werder Bremen	5
Thierry Henry Arsenal	5
Kaká AC Milan	5

▼ ALSO IN 2005/06

■ **Ballon d'Or**
Fabio Cannavaro
(Real Madrid)

■ **Mercury Music Prize** I Am A Bird Now

■ **BBC Sports Personality of the Year** Andrew Flintoff

■ **Oscar for best film** Crash

Considering how Barcelona dominate the modern game, it seems strange to comprehend that they were once considered perennial under-achievers in European competition and historically played second fiddle to mighty Real Madrid.

The 2005/06 Champions League campaign went some way to changing that image as Barcelona defeated Arsenal in the Stade de France, Paris, 50 years after the first European Cup final was won by Real Madrid.

This season's competition started controversially and somewhat early for holders Liverpool, who had lifted the trophy in dramatic circumstances against AC Milan in Istanbul. After finishing fifth in the English Premier League, they were refused entry to the competition to try to retain their crown under stringent UEFA guidelines that allowed only the top four teams in a domestic league to take part.

After the predictable public outcry, however, the suits at UEFA HQ in Nyon amended the rules and allowed Liverpool to join the Champions League in the first qualifying round. The Reds beat Total Network Solutions 6-0 on aggregate, FBK Kaunas 5-1 and CSKA Sofia 3-2 to reach the group stage, where they renewed their now-intense rivalry with José Mourinho's Chelsea. But topping the group was to be their last boastable action and they ran out of steam against Benfica in the last 16, losing 3-0 on aggregate.

Along with Chelsea and Liverpool, Arsenal, Juventus, Ajax, Barcelona and Inter qualified with their last game to spare. Manchester United, however, failed to progress from the group stage for the first time in 11 Champions

League seasons, surprisingly finishing bottom of Group D behind Lille, Benfica and tournament revelations Villareal, inspired by Juan Román Riquelme. Malcolm Glazer and sons – Manchester United's much-derided new American owners – couldn't even wave the flag in the UEFA Cup.

Arsenal's route to Paris was a tricky one – Real Madrid, Juventus and Villareal – but the combination of Cesc Fàbregas's vision and Thierry Henry's explosive pace and finishing meant they didn't have too many difficulties sweeping past *Los Blancos* or Italy's Old Lady. They beat Real Madrid 1-0 on aggregate with some organised defending and Juventus 2-0 on aggregate thanks to more of the same.

The semi-finals were a bit more of a struggle, though, and the north London side's outfield superstars required their influential German keeper Jens Lehmann to save a last-minute Riquelme penalty to propel the Gunners into the final.

Arsenal's route to Paris was tricky, but their sublime central combination of Fàbregas and Henry didn't have too many difficulties

▼ PLAYER OF THE TOURNAMENT

■ **Ronaldinho, Barcelona**
Pipping Arsenal's Thierry Henry by virtue of the final scoreline, Ronaldinho was the catalyst for the first Catalan European Cup success since 1991/92. He scored against Benfica in the quarter-final, laid on the only goal for Ludovic Giuly in the semi-final and his clever pass in the final forced Lehmann into making a red-card foul in the final.

Ronaldinho: A catalyst for the Catalans

THE FINAL

BARCELONA 2   1 ARSENAL

Eto'o 76,   Campbell 36
Belletti 80

Date 17 May 2006 **Stadium** Stade de France, Paris
Attendance 85,000 **Referee** Terje Hauge (Norway)

Undoubtedly the two best teams in Europe in 2005/06 were meeting in the final of the Champions League. There could be no question of that looking at the line-ups of Barcelona and Arsenal, their form and the way in which they had reached Paris.

Neither team had lost *any* of their 12 matches leading up to the final and, in Thierry Henry and Ronaldinho, they each had one of Europe's most feared strikers. But it wasn't to be quite the footballing exhibition that many had predicted and hoped for.

Dennis Bergkamp and Robin van Persie were eschewed by Arsène Wenger in favour of a more robust-looking, five-man midfield – but if either player had been on the pitch during the opening exchanges, Arsenal may have

cemented their domination.

As it was, after 39 minutes, a razor-sharp pass from Ronaldinho picked out Samuel Eto'o, who was brought down by Arsenal's semi-final hero Jens Lehmann, who was given his marching orders by Norwegian referee Terje Hauge.

Robert Pires had to be withdrawn to allow replacement keeper Manuel Almunia to come on and, afterwards, both managers agreed they would rather have seen Eto'o score, Lehmann be given a yellow card and the exhibition to continue.

Despite nothing coming of the free-kick and Arsenal going 1-0 up courtesy of Sol Campbell, the game never truly ignited the passions and late goals from Eto'o and Juliano Belletti broke the resolve of 10-man Arsenal.

THE LINE-UPS

V

Valdés, Oleguer (Belletti 70), Marquez, Puyol (c), Van Bronckhorst, Van Bommel (Larsson 60), Edmilson (Iniesta 46), Deco, Giuly, Ronaldinho, Eto'o | Lehmann, Eboué, Campbell, Touré, Cole, Hleb (Reyes 84), Fàbregas (Flamini 73), Gilberto Silva, Pires (Almunia 19) Ljungberg, Henry (c)

2006/07

A Milanese old-boy repays his manager's faith to fire his side to victory and serve up some sweet-tasting revenge for the *Rossoneri*

▼ DID YOU KNOW?

■ In January 2007, Michel Platini replaced Lennart Johansson as UEFA president, mostly thanks to votes from middle-ranking countries that supported his idea of trimming the top countries' Champions League entries. He has said that he wants to reduce the number of Spanish, English and Italian teams to a maximum of three, not four. Although, he has not stated when this will happen.

Platini: the Ballon d'Or winner three years in a row

▼ TOP GOALSCORERS

Kaká, AC Milan	**10**
Peter Crouch Liverpool	**6**
Ruud van Nistelrooy Real Madrid	**6**
Fernando Morientes Valencia	**6**
Didier Drogba Chelsea	**6**
Raúl González Real Madrid	**5**

▼ ALSO IN 2006/07

■ **Ballon d'Or**
Kaká (AC Milan)
■ **Mercury Music Prize** Whatever People Say I Am, That's What I'm Not
■ **BBC Sports Personality of the Year** Zara Phillips
■ **Oscar for best film** The Departed

Nothing could ever really make up for tossing away a three-goal lead against Liverpool in the 2004/05 final in Istanbul, after one of the greatest comebacks – and conversely, therefore, one of the greatest capitulations – European football has seen. But 2007's final provided some vengeful medicine for Carlo Ancelotti's restructured AC Milan.

Incredibly, an unfancied Italian side had gone all the way and won the 2006 World Cup in Germany, but the heroics of Marcelo Lippi's side shared the headlines with a much more unsanitary issue: the biggest match-fixing scandal in Italian football history. The upshot: Juventus, the country's best-loved club, were banished to Serie B and three of their defensive stars – Gianluca Zambrotta, Lilian Thuram and World Cup-winning captain Fabio Cannavaro – uprooted themselves to La Liga, to play for Barcelona or Real Madrid.

Heart of Midlothian's new heavy-handed benefactor, Lithuanian businessman Vladimir Romanov, felt the pinch as his befuddled bunch crashed out 5-1 to AEK Athens of Greece in the third qualifying round. Dinamo Zagreb suffered heavily at the hands of Arsenal; Fenerbahce went down to Dynamo Kyiv; and the once-almighty Ajax humiliatingly span into the first round of the UEFA Cup after a 3-2 defeat by Copenhagen.

Predictably, Sir Alex Ferguson's Manchester United recovered from a dismal showing the previous season to top Group F. They also helped Celtic to qualify by beating Benfica 1-0 in their last group match, thus eliminating the Portuguese and avenging the unexpected 2-1 away defeat that had

cost them so dear in December 2005.

There were dramatics at all the big English clubs – Arsenal, Liverpool and Manchester United were all under new ownership or in takeover talks with untrusted American benefactors, while Roman Abramovich's relationship with his most successful manager, José Mourinho, was near breaking point after the Chelsea owner sanctioned unnecessary purchases of Ukrainian Andriy Shevchenko and German captain Michael Ballack. But the Premier League's domination was clear for all to see.

An all-English final to match the Spanish and Italian affairs of 2000 and 2003 was only snuffed out by a superb semi-final, second-leg performance by Kaká to help AC Milan overturn Manchester United's 3-2 first-leg lead with a 3-0 win in the San Siro.

Abramovich, meanwhile, could only look on in anger as his heavily favoured Chelsea side lost to Liverpool, on penalties, for the second time in three years.

Abramovich could only look on in anger as his heavily favoured Chelsea side lost to Liverpool for the second time in three years

Kaká enjoyed his best season in Europe in 2006/07

THE FINAL

AC MILAN 2   1 LIVERPOOL
Inzaghi 45, 53   Kuyt 89

**Date 23 May 2007 Stadium Olympic Stadium, Athens
Attendance 85,000 Referee Herbert Fandel (Germany)**

Carlo Ancelotti recalled 33-year-old poacher Filippo Inzaghi to the starting line-up, in place of the younger, more mobile Alberto Gilardino – much to the surprise of pundits and so-called experts (but, come on, how often are these 'in-the-knows' actually right?).

The veteran striker provided the cutting edge in a close-fought victory that flew in the face of the Istanbul idiosyncrasies of 2004/05 and the Italian match-fixing scandal of 2006 that AC Milan were enveloped in.

Winger Jermaine Pennant proved an early thorn in Milan's side and should have put Liverpool ahead in the first half, but could only muster a lacklustre finish.

It was Inzaghi who, rather fortuitously, got the first goal of the game, putting the *Rossoneri* ahead against the run of play in the 45th minute. Replays showed the ball had struck his upper arm in the buildup to the goal, but the referee allowed it to stand.

Rafael Benítez's men regrouped and Istanbul hero Steven Gerrard should have levelled the scoreline, but his rather tame effort was well saved by Brazilian goalkeeper Dida.

It would be Milan's main man, Kaká, who would have the pivotal say in the Olympic Stadium, however, his incisive pass allowing Inzaghi to round Pepe Reina for a 2-0 cushion that Liverpool could not recover from this time around.

Milan had learned their lessons from 2005 and survived the worst domestic season in their proud footballing history by becoming the best team in Europe for the seventh time.

Football, eh?

THE LINE-UPS

**Dida, Oddo, Nesta, Maldini (c),
Jankulovski (Kaladze 78),
Gattuso, Pirlo, Ambrosini,
Seedorf (Favalli 90), Kaká,
Inzaghi (Gilardino 87)**

**Reina, Finnan (Arbeloa 87),
Carragher, Agger, Riise,
Pennant, Mascherano
(Crouch 77), Alonso, Zenden
(Kewell 58), Gerrard (c), Kuyt**

2007/08

It's a red night in Moscow as Ronaldo finds his feet to become a global superstar – but Terry takes a tumble at a crucial moment

▼ DID YOU KNOW?

■ A Champions League final ticket for Moscow on 21 May 2008 doubled as a short-term visa for fans to enter Russia, by order of president Vladimir Putin. The match was the first European Cup final staged in Russia.

■ Avram Grant was sacked as Chelsea boss three days after the final. During his widely criticised tenure, he did not lose a match at Stamford Bridge.

At least he beat Liverpool in Europe

▼ TOP GOALSCORERS

Cristiano Ronaldo Man United	**8**
Lionel Messi Barcelona	**6**
Fernando Torres Liverpool	**6**
Didier Drogba Chelsea	**6**
Steven Gerrard Liverpool	**6**
Ryan Babel Liverpool	**5**
Zlatan Ibrahimovic Inter	**5**
Frédéric Kanouté Sevilla	**5**

▼ ALSO IN 2007/08

■ **Ballon d'Or**
Cristiano Ronaldo (Man Utd)

■ **Mercury Music Prize** Myths Of The Near Future

■ **BBC Sports Personality of the Year** Joe Calzaghe

■ **Oscar for best film** No Country For Old Men

Ask a non-football type what 'CR7' is and they'll maybe guess it's a well-oiled machine, something foreign, probably European, quick and very expensive – and they'd be right, sort of.

Cristiano Ronaldo, Manchester United's über-slick Portuguese talisman, was certainly revved up in 2007/08 and, at the end of a busy, successful season, CR7 became shorthand for European Footballer of the Year and FIFA World Player of the Year – some achievement.

United began the tournament with a front three similar in setup to that of Spain in 2012. Each member of the triangle – Ronaldo, Wayne Rooney and Carlos Tevez – was mobile, good on the ball, able to beat a man and to apply a clinical finish. They were all equally comfortable up front or on either wing, and interchanged to devastating effect.

It had been 50 years since the Munich air disaster and 40 since George Best and co had lifted Manchester United's first European trophy, and Sir Alex Ferguson was determined to commemorate these events in the best way he knew how: by taking the club to glory again.

United topped Group F ahead of Roma, who left Ronaldo needing four stitches after their 1-0 defeat at Old Trafford and complained of his disrespectful showmanship after their 3-0 aggregate loss in the quarter-finals. In between, Ronaldo scored the crucial second-leg winner against Lyon in the Stade de Gerland.

Elsewhere, Liverpool bettered a good Inter side home (2-0) and away (0-1) to set up an intriguing tie with Arsenal, which Steven Gerrard settled

Luzhniki Stadium 21 May

with a decisive spot-kick. But the Reds' annual unravelling of Chelsea failed to materialise in the semi-finals.

Avram Grant successfully made the transition from the Blues' director of football to coach, despite the apparent protestations of some senior players, who claimed his coaching methods were 25 years out of date. Old-school or not, the Israeli did what the self-appointed 'Special One', José Mourinho, never had with Chelsea: beat Liverpool in Europe.

The Reds were belligerent to the end – despite John Arne Riise scoring an horrendous own goal in the first leg at Anfield – but Frank Lampard's penalty and a subsequent strike by Didier Drogba did for them in extra time of the second game.

Barcelona, shorn of Lionel Messi and Thierry Henry, couldn't hurt Manchester United in the other semi-final and a single strike from Paul Scholes meant the first all-English Champions League final was about to get under way.

CR7 was to become shorthand for European Fotballer of the Year and FIFA World Player of the Year – some achievement for the Portuguese

MAN UNITED 1   1 CHELSEA

Ronaldo 26   Lampard 45
AET United won 6-5 on penalties

Date **21 May 2008** Stadium **Luzhniki Stadium, Moscow**
Attendance **67,310** Referee **Lubos Michel (Slovakia)**

It doesn't take a genius to work out to whom Manchester United owed their path to the 2008 Champions League final – but, in the ultimate showdown, it was Sir Alex Ferguson's well-travelled goalkeeper, Edwin van der Sar, and not Cristiano Ronaldo who was the hero.

The Dutchman pointed to his left when Nicolas Anelka stepped up to take his spot-kick in another dramatic Champions League final shootout and then saved the Frenchman's effort to his right to secure a hard-earned victory.

Ronaldo did have his say early on, converting Wes Brown's cross with his head after a nice exchange of passes with Paul Scholes. Carlos Tevez and Michael Carrick then had decent opportunities to double the lead.

But Avram Grant's Chelsea side were nothing if not resilient and ever-present Frank Lampard capitalised on some loose defending by United to equalise just before the interval.

The second half belonged more to Chelsea: their Ivorian powerhouse striker Didier Drogba hit the post in the 77th minute and brought a fine save out of Van der Sar shortly afterwards.

One Red Devils veteran replaced another when Ryan Giggs came on for Scholes to make his 759th appearance for United, a club record. But he missed a chance to win the game in the dying seconds of normal time. Penalties were the inevitable result, and it was John Terry who sliced his effort wide, effectively costing Chelsea the title.

Van der Sar, Brown (Anderson 120), Ferdinand (c), Vidic, Evra, Hargreaves, Scholes (Giggs 87), Carrick, Ronaldo, Rooney (Nani 101), Tevez

Cech, Essien, Carvalho, Terry (c), A Cole, Makelele (Belletti 120), Ballack, Lampard, Drogba, J Cole (Anelka 99), Malouda (Kalou 92)

▼ PLAYER OF THE TOURNAMENT

■ **Cristiano Ronaldo, Manchester United**
In a forward line full of superstars (including Wayne Rooney and Carlos Tevez) Ronaldo stood out as superior. The Portuguese has pace in abundance, more tricks than Paul Daniels, can strike the ball cleanly with both feet and is domineering in the air. In short, he is the complete modern footballer.

Alex Ferguson's main man in 2007/08

2008/09

Chelsea feel hard done by and Sir Alex Ferguson's side are never really at the races as untouchable Messi cleans up with Barcelona

▼ **DID YOU KNOW?**

■ After being thrashed 4-0 by Liverpool in the second leg at Anfield, Real Madrid exited the Champions League in the round of 16 (first knockout round) for the fifth successive season.

■ Barcelona only had one attempt on target against Chelsea in their semi-final second-leg clash, but they scored from it and drew 1-1 – thereby progressing to make history.

"Yes, hi, can I have a taxi for Casillas, please?"

▼ **TOP GOALSCORERS**

Lionel Messi Barcelona	9
Steven Gerrard Liverpool	7
Miroslav Klose Bayern Munich	7
Lisandro López Porto	6
Emmanuel Adebayor Arsenal	5

▼ **ALSO IN 2008/09**

■ **Ballon d'Or**
Lionel Messi
(Barcelona)
■ **Mercury Music Prize** The Seldom Seen Kid
■ **BBC Sports Personality of the Year** Chris Hoy
■ **Oscar for best film** Slumdog Millionaire

By 27 May 2009, the short reign of CR7 was over. Barcelona were the new champions of Europe and their heartbeat was the untouchable, irresistible, diminutive Argentinian maestro, Lionel Messi: The Maradona of the Money Era. Unfortunately for the Portuguese prodigy, Messi's hold on the title of 'world's best' would only get tighter as the years went on.

This wasn't just a season for individual glory, though – it was the year Pep Guardiola's Barcelona announced their intentions to the planet and duly delivered. It is unlikely any other club will ever achieve what the 2009 Barça side did: the Champions League trophy, the La Liga title, the World Club Cup, the Spanish Cup, the Spanish Super Cup and the UEFA Super Cup. An astonishing yield of six trophies from six tournaments in 12 months. Quite remarkable.

Their Champions League triumph began in the third qualifying round on 13 August 2008 (Barcelona had only finished third in the Primera Division in 2007/08) with a routine 4-0 victory over Wisla Krakow, Samuel Eto'o scoring a hat-trick. Juventus beat Artmedia Petrzalka by the same score to seal their passage, while Dynamo Kyiv also found the net four times in their first-leg match to eventually cruise past Spartak Moscow 8-2. But Liverpool only won 0-1 against Standard Liege to scrape through.

UEFA president Michel Platini wanted to widen the scope of the tournament and his broader regime began to reap rewards in 2008/09 when four new teams reached the group stage – Denmark's Aalborg (who beat Celtic 2-1), Romania's CFR

Cluj (who beat Roma 1-2 at the Stadio Olimpico), Cyprus's Anorthosis (who beat Panathinaikos 3-1) and Belarus's Bate Borisov (who didn't beat anyone).

José Mourinho, now at Inter Milan, locked horns with old foe Sir Alex Ferguson in the first knockout round, the Scotsman avenging Manchester United's 2004 round-of-16 defeat by Porto with a 2-0 victory.

Barcelona scored five against Lyon in Camp Nou to eliminate the French side 6-3 on aggregate, while Bayern Munich trounced Sporting Lisbon 12-1 on aggregate and Liverpool beat Real Madrid 5-0 over two legs to send *Los Blancos* home at the round of 16.

Manchester United thrashed a buoyant Arsenal side 1-3 at the Emirates in their semi-final second leg to cruise into the final, but Barcelona limped across the line against Chelsea. They scored three minutes into stoppage time to go through on the away goal, referee Tom Henning Ovrebo ignoring yet another Chelsea penalty appeal in the final seconds.

The short reign of CR7 was over. Barça were the new champions of Europe and their heartbeat was the untouchable maestro Lionel Messi

The short reign of CR7 was over. Barça were the new champions of Europe and their heartbeat was the untouchable maestro Lionel Messi

▼ **PLAYER OF THE TOURNAMENT**

■ **Lionel Messi, Barcelona**
Already a player of some repute, Messi wasn't just picking the pockets of the smaller teams now – he was saving his most mesmeric, prolific performances for the weightiest opposition. Not only was he the highest scorer in the 2008/09 competition (see left), but he had a solid investment in many, many more.

Messi: plenty of reasons to smile in 2008/09

THE FINAL

BARCELONA 2   0 MAN UTD

Eto'o 10,
Messi 70

**Date 27 May 2009 Stadium Stadio Olimpico, Rome
Attendance 62,467 Referee Massimo Busacca (Switzerland)**

Again it seemed that the two best teams in Europe had conspired to lock horns in the continent's most lucrative match. We had Xavi and Andrés Iniesta comparing slide rules with Michael Carrick and Ryan Giggs, and we had the ultimate individual clashes: Thierry Henry versus Wayne Rooney and Lionel Messi versus Cristiano Ronaldo.

For a fifth year in a row, the final involved at least one English team and Manchester United were also the first defending champions to reach this stage since Juventus in 1997.

Tensions were suitably high, then – but despite Victor Valdés conceding a corner after just 10 seconds and then having to make a save from Ronaldo's free-kick, Catalan nerves settled first. After

10 minutes, Samuel Eto'o stabbed the ball past Edwin van der Sar after some classic short work by Messi and Iniesta.

Reeling from the goal, United began to squander possession and were glad of the break, Henry, Messi and Iniesta seemingly breaching their backline at will.

Carlos Tevez's introduction and a switch to 4-4-2 didn't help stem Barcelona's high-pressing game, with Rooney and Ronaldo failing to cut deep with their final passes. In the 70th minute, Barça's 5ft 7in Argentinian star *headed* the decisive goal, looping it over Van der Sar to seal victory.

United had missed Darren Fletcher's busying influence in midfield and not really been at the races. Their title was gone and CR7's crown had been dislodged.

THE LINE-UPS

Valdés, Puyol (c), Touré, Piqué, Sylvinho, Busquets, Xavi, Iniesta (Pedro 90), Messi, Henry (Keita 72), Eto'o

Van der Sar, O'Shea, Ferdinand, Vidic, Evra, Anderson (Tevez 46), Carrick, Giggs (c, Scholes 75), Park (Berbatov 66), Rooney, Ronaldo

2009/10

Mourinho does it again, this time in Italy, with an ageing Argentinian hitman being particularly responsive to his methods

▼ DID YOU KNOW?

■ In their first group-phase appearance, Russia's Rubin Kazan drew Barcelona and beat them in their own backyard, 1-2, thanks to goals from Aleksandr Ryazantsev and Gokdeniz Karadeniz.

■ The volcanic ash cloud from Iceland's Eyjafjallajokull forced Barcelona to get a coach to the San Siro for their semi-final first leg against Inter. José Mourinho could not have planned it better...

The *Tatary* celebrate a massive upset

▼ TOP GOALSCORERS

Lionel Messi Barcelona	8
Cristiano Ronaldo Real Madrid	7
Ivica Olic Bayern Munich	7
Diego Milito Inter	6
Nicklas Bendtner Arsenal	5
Wayne Rooney Man United	5
Marouane Chamakh Bordeaux	5

▼ ALSO IN 2009/10

■ **FIFA Ballon d'Or** Lionel Messi (Barcelona)

■ **Mercury Music Prize** Speech Therapy

■ **BBC Sports Personality of the Year** Ryan Giggs

■ **Oscar for best film** The Hurt Locker

Despite Europe being in the throes of recession – and many hundreds of clubs struggling to cope with the crippling wage structures they had burdened themselves with – Real Madrid were growing tired of under-achievement and living in the shadow of Barcelona. *Los Blancos*' chequebook was opened the widest it has ever been, to the tune of £140m, for just two players: £85m for Cristiano Ronaldo, from a reluctant Manchester United, and £55m for Kaká, from a significantly less reluctant Milan. But, to the amusement of the rest of the continent, Madrid would not even achieve their customary quarter-final exit, being dumped out unceremoniously in the round of 16 by Lyon, 2-1 on aggregate.

UEFA president Michel Platini was maintaining his efforts to widen the scope of the tournament to smaller, newer nations. The qualifying tournaments were now split into two groups: the Champions Path, for clubs who win their domestic league but who do not automatically qualify for the group stage (starting at the first qualifying stage) and the Non-Champions Path, for clubs who don't win their domestic league and who do not automatically qualify for the group stage (starting from the third qualifying round).

As a result of the new structure, group-stage debuts were handed to APOEL (Cyprus), AZ Alkmaar (Holland), Debrecen (Hungary), Rubin Kazan (Russia), Standard Liege (Belgium), Unirea Urziceni (Romania), Wolfsburg (Germany) and Zurich (Switzerland).

Bordeaux topped Group A ahead of heavyweights Bayern Munich and Juventus, and went all the way to the

quarter-finals before being knocked out by their countrymen, Lyon, 3-2 on aggregate. Chelsea cruised through Group D undefeated – joining Bordeaux as the only teams not to be conquered early in the competition – but Liverpool crashed out behind Fiorentina and Lyon in Group E, which was not really a surprise considering their alarming drop in domestic form.

Despite being drawn with Barcelona in the group stage and not scoring a goal past them – losing 2-0 and drawing 0-0 – José Mourinho had had 180 minutes in which to work out how his Inter side could beat the Catalans by the time they met again in the semi-finals. And beat them they did.

Mourinho had done for his old side Chelsea home and away in the last 16, and his tactical acumen proved just as astute in the San Siro, where Inter won 3-1, so a 1-0 defeat in Camp Nou was not enough to stop their progress.

Bayern smashed Lyon 4-0 on aggregate in the other semi-final, Arjen Robben continuing his fine form.

To the amusement of the rest of the continent, Madrid didn't even achieve their customary quarter-final exit, falling in the round of 16

▼ PLAYER OF THE TOURNAMENT

■ **Diego Milito, Inter**
The unlikeliest hero in a European season that was again supposed to be dominated by Pep Guardiola's brilliant Barcelona, Diego Milito shared the goalscoring limelight with his fellow Argentinian Lionel Messi in 2009 – and then stole it completely in the final by helping himself to two priceless goals. Brilliant.

Milito: the world's most clinical finisher in 2009

THE FINAL
INTER MILAN 2   0 BAYERN MUNICH
Milito 35, 70

Date 22 May 2010 **Stadium** Santiago Bernabéu
Attendance 73,170 **Referee** Howard Webb (England)

Neither finalist had come out on top in the group phase (Barcelona finished first in Inter's group and Bayern were bested by Bordeaux), which – if you consider the structure of the draw – means both had to fight doubly hard to get here. Needless to say, neither was about to roll over.

Inter Milan manager José Mourinho had worked as assistant to Bayern Munich's esteemed coach, Louis van Gaal, when he took over at Barcelona after Bobby Robson left. But now, in the Bernabéu, the student was aiming to overthrow the teacher.

Mourinho's plan was to concede possession to the Bavarians and hit them on the counter attack. It worked to great effect in the 35th minute, when a long clearance from Julio Cesar was nodded down by Diego Milito to Wesley Sneijder, whose return pass found the scampering Argentinian ready to beat Hans-Jörg Butt in the Munich goal

Inter's second goal wasn't quite so textbook, but still effective: Milito accepted Samuel Eto'o's pass before beating Daniel van Buyten and slotting home.

No Italian player would feature in Inter's line-up until Marco Materazzi came on in injury time, but the fans didn't care a jot. It was their first appearance in the final since 1972 and they had completed an unlikely league, cup and Champions League treble (a feat that Bayern would also have achieved had they lifted 'Big Ears'). Despite the likelihood of losing their Portuguese mastermind, they were going to celebrate.

THE LINE-UPS

Julio Cesar, Maicon, Lucio, Samuel, Chivu (Stankovic 68), Zanetti (c), Cambiasso, Eto'o, Sneijder, Pandev (Muntari 79), Milito (Materazzi 90)

Butt, Lahm, Van Buyten, Demichelis, Badstuber, Robben, Van Bommel (c), Schweinsteiger, Altintop (Klose 63), Müller, Olic (Gomez 74)

2010/11

The rest of Europe go back to the drawing board as Pep Guardiola's footballing philosophy is put into practice to devastating effect

▼ DID YOU KNOW?

■ This Champions League final was only the second to be played on a Saturday night. UEFA president Michel Platini had moved it to the weekend hoping to gain a wider audience. It worked, with 109m viewers worldwide.

■ Barcelona have beaten English teams in all three of their Champions League finals: 2006 – Arsenal; and 2011 and 2009 – Manchester United.

Arsenal bite Catalonian dust back in 2006

▼ TOP GOALSCORERS

Lionel Messi Barcelona	12
Mario Gomez Bayern Munich	8
Samuel Eto'o Inter	8
Nicolas Anelka Chelsea	7
Karim Benzema Real Madrid	6
Roberto Soldado Valencia	6
Cristiano Ronaldo Real Madrid	6

▼ ALSO IN 2010/11

■ **FIFA Ballon d'Or** Lionel Messi (Barcelona)

■ **Mercury Music Prize** The xx

■ **BBC Sports Personality of the Year** Tony McCoy

■ **Oscar for best film** The King's Speech

Being a perfectionist isn't easy. Despite his side playing effortless, elegant football throughout the 2010/11 Champions League campaign – and overcoming hated rivals Real Madrid in the semi-finals – Barcelona manager Pep Guardiola made it clear before the final that he wanted to see vast improvements on the 2008/09 showpiece, when he believed the true Catalan spirit was not in evidence. He wanted to right that wrong and to show the world what his footballing philosophy was truly about.

Nine months earlier, the line-up of the group stage was being finalised through qualifying and the play-offs, with Ukrainian giants Dynamo Kyiv falling short, 3-2 on aggregate against Ajax. Celtic flopped to eventual Europa League finalists Braga; Rosenborg lost on away goals to Scandinavian rivals Copenhagen; and Harry Redknapp's Spurs recovered from a 3-2 defeat by Young Boys in Bern to thump the Swiss 4-0 at White Hart Lane and begin a memorable campaign.

Despite a slow start to the group stage by the north London side, drawing 2-2 with Werder Bremen and going 4-0 down against Inter, a second-half hat-trick by Gareth Bale in the San Siro made the scoreline respectable and gave Spurs the confidence to beat the holders at home. They went on to top the group by a point. Their fearless attacking spirit had gained momentum on the domestic front and now it, and Bale, had admirers on the continent, too.

In the round of 16, Spurs knocked out AC Milan 1-0 on aggregate, Peter Crouch scoring in the San Siro, but they collapsed in the Bernabéu to José

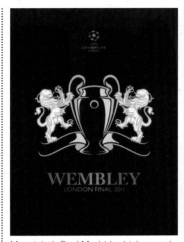

Mourinho's Real Madrid, which meant they had an insurmountable four goals to overturn in the second leg.

Madrid's philosophy and Mourinho's tactics hadn't seemed to fit at first, but the partnership was beginning to produce results. Fiery semi-final clashes with free-scoring Barcelona were decided by the artistry of Lionel Messi, who scored twice in Spain's capital city, which allowed his team-mates to play keep-ball in the second leg at Camp Nou – but Mourinho was beginning to learn how to crack the Catalan spirit.

Manchester United were in no mood to succumb either. They topped Group C undefeated and went on to conquer Marseille (2-1), Chelsea (3-1) and Schalke 04 (6-1) without conceding an away goal, en route to another Champions League final clash with Guardiola's Barça.

A hugely entertaining buildup then to what promised to be another classic final. Would Sir Alex Ferguson have the answers this time?

Guardiola made it clear he wanted vast improvements on the 2008/09 showpiece... he wanted to show the world what his philosophy was about

THE FINAL

BARCELONA 3   1 MAN UTD

Pedro 27,   Rooney 34
Messi 54, Villa 69

**Date 28 May 2011 Stadium Wembley Stadium, London
Attendance 87,695 Referee Viktor Kassai (Hungary)**

Both 2010/11 finalists went into the game with three European Cups under their belts. But after making a sharp start, it quickly became clear that Manchester United's inferior gameplan would make it mighty difficult for them to add to their tally.

David Villa had a couple of shots as Barça began to control the game and command the ball, and, in the 27th minute, Xavi found Pedro on the edge of the box. He let fly with a shot past Edwin van der Sar for the opener.

Somewhat against the run of play, Wayne Rooney equalised, executing a smart one-two with Ryan Giggs before curling in a shot from 15 yards out. But it signalled a momentary lapse in concentration by Pep Guardiola's men, rather than a shift in momentum, and

Lionel Messi and co looked menacing again before half-time.

Barça resumed control after the break and began to pester a hitherto resilient United. They regained the lead in the 54th minute, when Messi fired in a shot from 20 yards out, and they extended their lead 15 minutes later. Villa received the ball a similar distance from goal and curled a glorious shot into the top corner of United's net. Superiority assured, the rest of the game was comfortably played out.

Barcelona joined Ajax and Bayern Munich in winning Europe's premier competition four times and Guardiola had been sated. The Champions League had become the world's most-watched annual sports event and *his* team were doing the entertaining.

THE LINE-UPS

V

Valdés, Alves (Puyol 88), Mascherano, Piqué, Abidal, Xavi (c), Busquets, Iniesta, Villa (Keita 86), Messi, Pedro (Afellay 90)

Van der Sar, Fabio da Silva (Nani 69), Ferdinand, Vidic (c), Evra, Valencia, Carrick (Scholes 77), Giggs, Park, Rooney, Hernández

▼ PLAYER OF THE TOURNAMENT

■ **Lionel Messi, Barcelona**
Aside from local artillery or illegal barricading, there was no stopping Lionel Messi in 2010/11. Under instruction from Pep Guardiola to become the player everyone at Barça knew he could be, the Argentinian flourished and weighed in with his highest tally of goals to date. An unremitting force of footballing nature.

If he plays well, Barça usually win. Simple.

2011/12

El Clásico fails to materialise, but Didier Drogba stars in a dramatic denouement to deliver Chelsea owner's first European trophy

▼ **DID YOU KNOW?**

■ As part of a UEFA initiative, two extra match officials – one behind each goal – were used for the first time in 2011/12, from the play-off rounds to the final.

■ German ex-footballer Paul Breitner was the official ambassador for the 2011/12 final, and is one of only four footballers to have scored in two World Cup finals (the others being Zinedine Zidane, Pelé and Vavá).

Breitner lining up for West Germany in 1982

▼ **TOP GOALSCORERS**

Lionel Messi Barcelona		14
Mario Gomez Bayern Munich		12
Cristiano Ronaldo Real Madrid		10
Karim Benzema Real Madrid		7
Didier Drogba Chelsea		6

▼ **ALSO IN 2011/12**

■ **FIFA Ballon d'Or**
Lionel Messi
(Barcelona)

■ **Mercury Music Prize**
Let England Shake

■ **BBC Sports Personality of the Year** Mark Cavendish

■ **Oscar for best film** The Artist

And so to the 20th season of the best club football competition in the world. Since Marseille astonished AC Milan by winning the inaugural competition in 1992/93, UEFA's principal tournament has forever changed football across the continent.

The Champions League final is now the most watched annual sporting event on the planet and its earning potential has irrevocably changed the domestic leagues that service the competition. How fitting then, when we talk of change, that the final of 2011/12 was staged in one of the most modern stadiums in Europe and won by one of football's new superpowers.

It began on 28 June 2011 with Valletta of Malta and F91 Dudelange of Luxembourg winning their first qualifying matches away to Tre Fiori, of San Marino, and FCSanta Coloma, of Andorra, respectively.

Arsenal got a tough draw in the play-offs, but saw off Udinese 3-1 on aggregate; Sturm Graz were sent packing by determined Belarussians, BATE Borisov; and Barcelona-tormentors Rubin Kazan were denied entry to the group stages by a well-prepared Lyon.

Manchester City, now owned by Sheikh Mansour, of the Abu Dhabi royal family, were making their first appearance in the tournament and expected to do well considering their new owner had pumped £500m into buying the world's best players. But it wasn't to be for Roberto Mancini's mob of millionaires. Drawn in a group with no 'easy' ties, they twice beat a Villareal in decline, but defeats in Naples and Munich cost them dear. Shockingly,

Manchester United, in a comparatively weak group with Benfica, Basel and Otelul Galati, also went out.

Elsewhere, Benfica and champions Barcelona remained undefeated in groups C and H; José Mourinho's Real Madrid won all of their matches in Group D, scoring 19 goals; and German champions Borussia Dortmund finished bottom of Group F, only managing to beat Olympiacos.

Arsenal's 4-0, round-of-16, first-leg defeat by Milan in the San Siro effectively ended their challenge, despite a face-saving 3-0 win in the second leg, and Chelsea used all 120 minutes of their second leg to squeeze past Napoli 5-4. A 3-1 aggregate victory over Benfica proved much simpler, which left a semi-final line-up of Munich v Madrid and Chelsea v Barcelona, most analysts predicting an *El Clásico* 20th anniversary match.

But Ramires and Fernando Torres did for the Catalans in Camp Nou and Mourinho's march was ended by the German side, 3-1 on penalties.

THE FINAL

CHELSEA 1   1 BAYERN MUNICH

Drogba 88   Müller 83
AET Chelsea won 4-3 on penalties

Date **19 May 2012** Stadium **Allianz Arena, Munich**
Attendance **62,500** Referee **Pedro Proença (Portugal)**

Chelsea set themselves up in much the same way as they had done against Barcelona in the semi-final. It was not a tactic appealing to purists, with 10 men slotted in behind the ball, but it again turned out to be effective.

For most of the game, the Blues conceded possession to Bayern Munich, but wave after wave of Bavarian attacks were thwarted and countless chances wasted in front of home support. However, just when it looked as if Chelsea would take the game to extra time, Thomas Müller connected with Toni Kroos' centre to give Bayern the lead in the 83rd minute.

But the drama hadn't ended. Müller gave way to Daniel van Buyten as Bayern attempted to shore up their backline, but Chelsea's Didier Drogba wriggled free and pumped a header, from Juan Mata's corner, past keeper Manuel Neuer to equalise.

In extra time, Drogba fouled French winger Franck Ribéry to give away a stupid penalty, but Petr Cech came to the Ivorian's rescue by saving Arjen Robben's weak effort from the spot.

Drogba would atone when the game moved into the dreaded penalty shootout. Mata missed Chelsea's first kick, but Bayern's substitute striker Ivica Olic and club captain Bastian Schweinsteiger also missed their penalties, giving Drogba the chance to win the game – and he made no mistake. They didn't play the beautiful football that owner Roman Abramovich covets, but Chelsea were European champions for the first time.

It wasn't to be for Mancini's mob of millionaires. Despite beating Villareal twice, away defeats in Naples and Munich cost them dear

▼ PLAYER OF THE TOURNAMENT

■ **Didier Drogba, Chelsea**
The Marmite of modern footballers, dazzling Drogba has strength and impudence, power and control, courage and imagination; enough qualities to counter the other side of his character – petulance, theatrics and simulation. Throughout 2011/12 he got the balance right and his just desserts: a Champions League title.

Drogba: you either love him or hate him

THE LINE-UPS

Cech, Bosingwa, Luiz, Cahill, Cole, Mikel, Lampard (c), Kalou (Torres 84), Mata, Bertrand (Malouda 73), Drogba

Neuer, Lahm (c), Boateng, Tymoshchuk, Contento, Schweinsteiger, Kroos, Robben, Müller (Van Buyten 87), Ribéry (Olic 97), Gomez

EXTRA
TIME

TOP 10
MEMORABLE MOMENTS

Extraordinary instances
that have stuck in the
mind of the continent

Dudek saves Reds
Liverpool v AC Milan, 2004/05

1 Epitomising the madness of the best
Champions League final ever – and
just pipping his do-or-die, extra-time
double save from Andriy Shevchenko – this
title-winning penalty stop carved Jerzy Dudek's
name into Anfield folklore. Adopting the 'rubbery
leg' distraction tactic used by legendary
Reds keeper Bruce Grobbelaar, Dudek put off
Shevchenko, saved the spot-kick and sealed the
greatest comeback in the tournament's history.

Quick 'un Ricken
Borussia Dortmund v Juventus, 1996/97

5 Talk about impact substitution. Borussia
Dortmund were 2-1 up when 20-year-old
wunderkind Lars Ricken was brought on
as a fresh pair of legs after 71 minutes. Within a
lightning 15 seconds he had scored a delightful goal,
running on to a slide-rule pass before lobbing the
helpless Juventus keeper with a frightening degree
of collection. Ricken was born in Dortmund and
had played at the club since the start of his career –
which made the goal that bit more special.

Yes we Kahn!
Bayern Munich v Valencia, 2000/01

6 The San Siro was the backdrop for this
epic final, which – at 1-1 after normal and
extra time – headed into the uncertainty
of a penalty shootout. Valencia keeper Santiago
Canizares saved two spot-kicks, but Bayern's
Oliver Kahn, in his pomp, was not to be outdone.
He saved three to secure the German side's
first Champions League title and the man of the
match award – the first time the accolade had
been awarded to a goalkeeper.

José who?
Manchester Utd v Porto, 2009/10

7 Not many people would have heard of José
Mourinho before Porto played the Red
Devils at Old Trafford in the second leg of
the last 16. Porto needed a draw to proceed in the
competition and draw they did, midfielder Costinha
scoring on 90 minutes to take the Portuguese side
through 3-2 on aggregate. Mourinho charged down
the touchline, celebrating as if he'd scored the goal
himself. Porto went on to win the competition and a
certain Roman Abramovich took note.

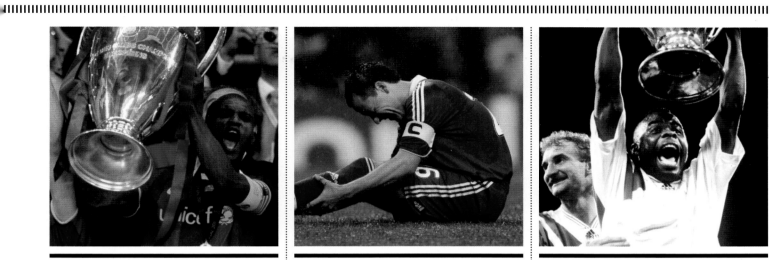

Abidal lifts the trophy
Barcelona v Manchester Utd, 2010/11

2 Only two-and-a-half months after enduring a three-hour operation to remove a cancerous tumour from his liver, French defender Eric Abidal was chosen to lift the trophy after Barça's 3-1 victory over the Red Devils in the 2010/11 final – having played the full 90 minutes. In front of 85,000 fans in Wembley stadium, Carles Puyol first handed Abidal the skipper's armband and then the trophy to lift. An emotional tribute to an exceptional player.

Terry off target
Manchester Utd v Chelsea, 2007/08

3 Didier Drogba had been sent off earlier in the game for a petulant slap on Nemanja Vidic, so Chelsea needed an additional penalty-taker once extra time had ended in stalemate. Up stood 'Mr Chelsea', John Terry. Unfortunately, he wasn't standing for long. A rainstorm had produced an extremely slippery playing surface in Moscow's Luzhniki stadium, and Terry's standing foot slid as he struck the ball, causing it to rocket wide.

Boli on the ball
Marseille v AC Milan, 1992/93

4 The first Champions League final – and with the likes of Van Basten, Rijkaard, Rossi and Maldini in their ranks, everyone was expecting an AC Milan rout. What the footballing world wasn't expecting was Basile Boli's well-worked header (from a corner) after 43 minutes, which not only gave Marseille the lead, but ultimately secured them the inaugural Champions League trophy. Unfortunately for the French side, they have not enjoyed success at such a level since.

Rampant Ronaldo
Manchester Utd v Real Madrid, 2002/03

8 In the pantheon of Champions League performances, Ronaldo's hat-trick at Old Trafford ranks as one of the greatest. United fought hard, with Ruud van Nistelrooy and David Beckham scoring against their future club, but the Brazilian was unplayable and received a standing ovation from both sets of fans when he was substituted. Zinedine Zidane, Fernando Redondo and Steve McManaman were also magnificent for Real.

Zidane the master
Bayer Leverkusen v Real Madrid, 2001/02

9 There are flashy volleys, opportunistic volleys and flukey volleys, but all pale in comparison to Zinedine Zidane's beautifully engineered volley against Bayer Leverkusen at Hampden Park in the 2001/02 final. A deflected cross from the left looped in-field, and seemed to hang forever before being met by the perfectly positioned (weaker!) left foot of Zidane. The resulting goal is a thing of rare beauty, technique and execution – and it secured Zidane's reputation as a genius.

Comeback kings
Manchester Utd v Bayern Munich, 1998/99

10 When Manchester United reached the 1998/99 final, they were already proud holders of the Premier League title and the FA Cup. Victory over Bayern would secure their first Treble. After 90 minutes, this looked unlikely, especially as Bayern led through a sixth-minute goal from Mario Basler. But United substitutes Teddy Sheringham and Ole Gunnar Solskjaer scored in the 90th and 92nd minutes respectively to secure an incredible victory.

Marseille
1992/93

French football has yet to repeat the feat of these intrepid inaugural winners (either on the pitch or off it)

1 Bernard Casoni
Casoni stayed at Marseille until 1996 when, after 169 appearances, he called time on his playing career. After a couple of years off, he was back in football as a manager, his most successful stint being with French side Evian Thonon Gaillard, whom he helped to two successive promotions between 2010 and 2012. Casoni mow manages Club Africain in Tunisia.

2 Eric Di Meco
A season after Marseille's Champions League trial, continuing financial difficulties resulted in the club being relegated two divisions, which prompted Di Meco to move on – to Monaco. He played out the final years of his career there, finally retiring in 1998 at the age of 35 – but not before adding a league title in 1997.

3 Marcel Desailly
Desailly moved to Milan in 1993, where he won the Champions League again in 1994, plus Serie A titles in that year and 1996. In 1998, he moved to Chelsea, winning the FA Cup in 2000 before heading to Qatar in 2004 to play for Al-Gharafa. He helped them to win the Qatar League in 2005, moved to Qatar SC in the same year, and retired in 2006.

4 Basile Boli
Boli left Marseille in 1994 (but only after recording *We've Got A Feeling* **with team-mate Chris Waddle – the video has to be seen to be believed) and spent a season each at Rangers, Monaco and Japanese side Urawa Red Diamonds before retiring in 1997. He's also famous for nutting Stuart Pearce when playing for France in Euro '92. A brave/ill-informed man.**

5 Didier Deschamps
After moving to Juventus in 1994, Deschamps won the Champions League again in 1996, while a move to Chelsea in 1999 brought an FA Cup winner's medal. He ended his playing career at Valencia in 2001 and went into management with Monaco (with whom he won the league in 2003), Juventus (promotion to La Liga in 2007) and Marseille, eventually earning the top job with the French national team in 2012.

6 Abedi Pele
One of the first African players to make an impact in Europe, Pele moved to Lyon in 1993, then Turin and Munich 1860 before retiring from playing while at Al Ain (UAE) in 2000. An ambassador for Ghanaian football, he is also the chairman/coach of Ghanaian Division 1 side Nania FC.

THE BIG ONE

Every club across Europe has their sights set on 'Big Ears'

The UEFA Champions League trophy – also known as the European Champion Clubs' Cup, the Coupe des Clubs Champions Européens or, simply, the European Cup – is the most coveted club trophy on the planet. It represents the pinnacle of footballing achievement for club sides on the continent and the showpiece final has become the world's most-watched annual sporting event.

During the 1968/69 campaign, it was decreed that any club who won the championship five times in total or three times in succession could keep the trophy and another would be moulded for the next term.

The original trophy was used until 1966 and then awarded permanently to Real Madrid in 1967 in honour of their six victories, including five on the bounce after the competition's inception in 1955.

Celtic were the first team, in 1967, to win the new trophy, which the Spanish nicknamed *La Orejona* ('big ears') because of its wonderfully oversized handles. It was designed and made by Jorge Stadelmann, a jeweller from the Swiss capital Bern, who incorporated elements of design that would appeal to nations across the continent.

Since 2009, winning teams are only given a replica, with their names engraved upon it, the original being kept at UEFA headquarters in Nyon, Switzerland. Previously, the winning club would have kept the real trophy for 10 months before receiving a scaled-down replica.

There are currently only five clubs who have been allowed to keep the trophy under the rules adhered to between 1968/69 and 2008/09. They are:

■ **Real Madrid, after winning the first five European club tournaments between 1956 and 1960, and again in 1966.** *Los Blancos* **have won three more times since, in 1998, 2000, and 2002;**

■ **Ajax, who won the tournament three times in a row from 1971-73. They won a fourth title in 1995;**

■ **Bayern Munich, who won three consecutive European Cups from 1974-76 and a fourth in 2001;**

■ **AC Milan, after winning their fifth title in 1994. They have since won the Champions League twice more, in 2003 and 2007;**

■ **and Liverpool, after claiming their fifth title in 2005.**

TOP 10
GREATEST
MANAGERS

They came, they saw, they
conquered – they tried again

Sir Alex Ferguson

1 What is there to say about Sir Alex Ferguson that hasn't been said already? One of the most successful club managers ever, his phenomenal Manchester United record of 12 English Premier League titles, five FA Cups and four league cups is rounded off nicely by two Champions League victories. Of 194 European games played, he has lost only 43.

Ottmar Hitzfeld

5 One of Europe's greats, the indomitable Herr Hitzfeld is a true Germanic legend. Having revived Borussia Dortmund in the mid-1990s (a stint that included a Champions League title in 1997), Bayern Munich came calling and he quickly secured four Bundesliga titles in Bavaria. In 2001, he became only the second coach to win the Champions League with two clubs.

Vicente del Bosque

6 A Real Madrid playing legend, it wasn't until 1999 that Del Bosque took full managerial control at the Bernabéu. Success quickly followed and he won La Liga in 2000/01 and 2002/03, and also secured the Champions League trophy in 1999/2000 and 2001/02. He has since enjoyed moderate success with the Spanish national team...

Pep Guardiola

7 A glittering playing career with Barcelona was followed by the dugout hotseat in 2008. With the help of Messrs Xavi, Iniesta and Messi, Guardiola crafted a bunch of highly talented players into what is generally considered to be the best team ever to have existed. He won two Champions League titles with them, in 2008/09 and 2010/11, before stepping down in 2012.

José Mourinho

2 The 'Special One' has an enviable record in domestic and European competitions. He has won league titles with Porto, Chelsea, Inter Milan and Real Madrid, and secured the Champions League with Porto and Inter. He wasn't able to deliver Europe's top prize for Blues owner Roman Abramovich and has yet to do so at Real Madrid – but it can only be a matter of time.

Rafa Benítez

3 Although a decent player, Rafael Benítez ultimately found his calling in the dugout, and he has long been considered one of the game's sharpest tacticians. His greatest achievement to date is winning the Champions League with Liverpool in 2005, a final often referred to as 'The Miracle of Istanbul' because of Liverpool's Houdini-style comeback.

Carlo Ancelotti

4 So much more than the greatest left eyebrow in football, Carlo Ancelotti has enjoyed significant success at some of the world's greatest clubs, including Juventus, AC Milan and Chelsea. He secured the English Premier League and FA Cup with the Blues, while delivering two Champions League trophies to Milan, in 2002/03 and 2006/07. A real master.

Louis van Gaal

8 An avid proponent of Total Football, Van Gaal started his managerial career at Ajax, with whom he spent six years collecting the top trophies in Dutch and European football, including the Champions League in 1995. Spells with Barcelona, the Dutch national team and Bayern Munich followed, before a return to coaching the national side.

Marcello Lippi

9 The Italian regularly features in 'top 10 greatest manager' lists and a brief glance at his record will tell you why. Much of his club success came at Juventus, with whom he won the Champions League in 1996 and finished as runners-up in 1997, 1998 and 2003. But possibly his proudest moment was winning the 2006 World Cup with Italy. Now manages Chinese side Guangzhou Evergrande.

Fabio Capello

10 The austere Mr Capello will be fondly remembered in the UK for his years as England manager... but he's been a massive name in Europe for years. Amazingly, he's won the domestic league with every team he has managed – lifting the Serie A crown six times and La Liga twice – and secured the Champions League for AC Milan in 1994.

Ajax
1994/95

They were the young guns who shocked AC Milan in Vienna – but did they go on to be big shots?

1 Finidi George
After the highs of 1995, George moved to Spanish side Real Betis in 1996 and stayed there for four years, hitting double figures in nearly every season. He spent the 2000/01 season at Mallorca before transferring to Ipswich Town for two years from 2001 to 2003. However, the move wasn't a massive success and he moved back to Mallorca for a season before retiring.

2 Michael Reiziger
Like Finidi George, Reiziger departed Ajax in 1996, but for AC Milan. An injury-hit season prompted a move to Louis Van Gaal's Barcelona, where he stayed until 2004, securing two La Liga titles in the process. The Premier League and Middlesbrough then called, but more injury woe led to Reiziger leaving for PSV in 2005, where he retired after two seasons.

3 Marc Overmars
Overmars moved to Arsenal in 1997 and helped the Gunners to a league and cup double in his first season. Barcelona came calling in 2000 and he became a regular starter for them before retiring in 2004 because of injury. Overmars joined Dutch side Go Ahead Eagles as technical director and, in 2012, became Ajax's director of football.

4 Nwankwo Kanu
The legendary Nigerian moved to Inter in 1996, but his time in Italy was disrupted by a heart problem and, in 1999, he moved to Arsenal. He made an immediate impact with the Gunners, especially as a 'super sub', and won the Double in 2002, the FA Cup in 2003 and the Premier League in 2004. Two seasons with West Brom followed, before a move to Portsmouth, with whom he also won the FA Cup in 2008.

5 Winston Bogarde
Bogarde moved to AC Milan in 1997 and then to Barcelona (under Van Gaal) in 1998. He famously moved to Chelsea in 2000 on a then ludicrous wage (allegedly around £40,000 a week) and was ridiculed for making only four appearances for The Blues in four years, happy to cash in rather than find game time elsewhere. He retired in 2004.

6 Danny Blind
Blind ended his playing career at Ajax in 1999. He spent a season as the club's manager (2005/06) before moving to Sparta Rotterdam as technical director. But he was soon back at Ajax (in various roles) and, in 2012, became assistant coach of the national team under Van Gaal.

18 years 335 days

Wayne Rooney's age when he became the youngest scorer of a Champions League hat-trick against Fenerbahce on 28 September 2004

10.12 seconds

Time taken to score the fastest goal in the Champions League, by Bayern Munich's Roy Makaay against Real Madrid on 7 March 2007

20

The most goals scored in a group stage, by Manchester United in 1998/99 and by Barcelona in 2011/12

CHAMPIONS LEAGUE

10
Most consecutive clean sheets in the CL, by Arsenal in 2005/06

481
Minutes from the start of the campaign in which Manchester United did not concede a single goal in 2010/11

18
The number of times Manchester United have competed in the CL, more than any other club

7-0
The largest margin of victory in the Champions League knockout rounds, Bayern Munich thrashing Basel in the first knockout round in 2011/12

4
Number of consecutive times Lionel Messi has won the Champions League top scorer award: 2008/09, 2009/10, 2010/11 and 2011/12

10
Number of Portuguese players in Porto's starting line-up when they won the 2004 final

16
Number of CL seasons in which Manchester United's Ryan Giggs has scored

0
Number of teams that have managed to defend their Champions League crown

200 million

Number of people from the Far East alone who tuned in to watch the 2011/12 group stage

300 million+

UEFA's estimate of how many people across the globe watch the Champions League final on television

4.8 million

Number of Champions League-related tweets made during the 2011/12 final between Bayern Munich and Chelsea

£42m

The amount Chelsea are thought to have earned after winning the Champions League title in 2012

6

Number of times the Champions League winners have not actually been winners of their domestic league. Manchester United (1999), Real Madrid (2000), AC Milan (2003 and 2007), Liverpool (2005), Barcelona (2009) and Chelsea (2012).

IN NUMBERS

Figure out what makes Europe's greatest club competition so great

31

Longest unbeaten CL run at home, by Bayern Munich, which ended with a 2-3 defeat by Deportivo La Coruna in the first group stage in 2002/03

25

Longest undefeated run in the Champions League, by Manchester United – beginning with a 1-0 win against Sporting in the opening group game of 2007/08. It was halted by 0-2 defeat by Barcelona in the final

10-0

Largest victory in the CL era, HJK Helsinki beating Bangor City in the second qualifying round in 2011/12

3

Times the final has been contested by teams from the same country: 2000 Spain (Real Madrid 3–0 Valencia); 2003 Italy (Milan 0–0 Juventus, 3-2 on pens) and 2008 England (Manchester United 1–1 Chelsea, 6-5 on pens)

37 years 289 days

Ryan Giggs' age when he scored a Champions League goal against Benfica on 14 September 2011, to become the oldest player to hit the net in the competition

TOP 10
DODGY
HAIRCUTS

Some players like to put their barber (or lack of one) in the spotlight alongside their skills

Carles Puyol
Barcelona

1 A clear disciple of the Karel Poborsky school of hair, this mop hasn't impeded Puyol's stellar career.

Karel Poborsky
Manchester United

5 Fairly reprehensible, washed-out, extra-split Central European version of 'the Claudio Cannigia'. A weighty mess.

Taribo West
Internazionale

6 Indescribable 'style' that Mr West sported for almost his entire career. Points for perseverance.

Jari Litmanen
Ajax

7 A hairdo sported by Hollywood's greatest female leads during the early/mid-1990s. Says it all really.

Bacary Sagna
Arsenal

2 Sagna's hairdo looks as if it's attacking him or the result of some botched biological experiment. Not great either way.

Moreno Torricelli
Juventus

3 Torricelli's theatrical playing style was mirrored by his slightly hysterical bouffant and matching lip-wear.

Rudi Völler
Marseille

4 Power, grace, style and finesse... and that's just Völler's perm-moustache combo. He's still rocking a whiter version today.

Abel Xavier
Liverpool

8 No stranger to a bottle of Domestos and a second-hand super-hero comic, Abel Xavier had a style all of his own.

Gervinho
Arsenal

9 A second entry for Arsenal – and one of the most receding hairlines to grace the field. It literally goes *all* the way back.

Roberto Baggio
Milan

10 Baggio was known as 'The Divine Ponytail' throughout his acclaimed career. Divine might be pushing it.

Man Utd
1998/99

The future stories of a team that could never be written off

1 Jonathan Greening
A remarkably fresh-faced Greening ultimately struggled to find regular football with the Red Devils and followed Steve McClaren to Middlesbrough in 2001. In 2004, he moved to West Brom and went on to captain the side from midfield, until he was loaned to Fulham in 2009. He played a solid role in helping the Cottagers to the Europa League final that season, but departed for Nottingham Forest in 2011.

2 David Beckham
Unappreciative of his ballooning media profile, Sir Alex Ferguson sold David Beckham to Real Madrid in 2003 to join up with the mega-bucks Galacticos where he eventually won La Liga in 2006/07. Another lucrative contract with LA Galaxy followed, and in 2011 he helped *Los Galacticos* win the MLS Cup.

3 David May
The rise of Gary Neville and Wes Brown, and the purchase of Henning Berg, led to fewer first-team opportunities for May, who went on loan to Huddersfield before signing for Burnley on a free transfer in 2003. His career was blighted by injuries and he retired in 2006, having played his last season for non-league outfit Bacup Borough. May has the dubious honour of ranking 43rd in the *Times'* list of worst-ever footballers and since retirement has been teaching football to kids in Dubai. He also runs his own wine import company.

4 Teddy Sheringham
Sheringham had become a fans' favourite by 2003, when he left Manchester United for Portsmouth (where he became the oldest Premiership scorer of a hat-trick). A season later, at the age of 38, he moved to Championship side West Ham and helped them to secure promotion. He finished his playing career (having broken a host of age-related records) at Colchester United in 2008.

5 Jesper Blomqvist
A rousing performance in the 1999 Champions League final was followed by two years of injury misery for Blomqvist, during which time he didn't play at all (leaving him plenty of time to present 'Cooking With Jesper' on MUTV). Short spells with Everton and Charlton followed, before a return to Sweden, where he was again plagued by injuries. Retirement called in 2005 and he turned to coaching in 2008, occasionally playing as a substitute. In 2012, Blomqvist hung up his boots for good and began a course in commerce.

6 Ronny Johnsen
After a trophy-sprinkled six years with Manchester United, Johnsen moved to Aston Villa in 2002, for a two-season stint. This was followed by a year at Newcastle, but the Magpies let him go in 2005. He initially decided to retire, but then returned to play for Norwegian outfit Valerenga between 2005 and 2008.

Firsts & Lasts

Significant yardsticks and weighty barometers from 20 remarkable years of Europe's biggest club competition

1992/93

■ **1992/93 was the 38th European Cup overall, but the competition's first season in the guise of the UEFA Champions League**

■ It was the first Champions League season since the break-up of the USSR and Yugoslavia. This resulted in a large number of new countries eligible to enter their champions into the competition and the inevitable restructuring of the tournament to include a preliminary round

■ **The Champions League was won by Marseille, the first and only time a French club has achieved the feat**

■ Barcelona were the last team to win the European Champions' Club Cup before it became the UEFA Champions League, in 1991/92. They were eliminated in the first Champions League tournament, 4-3 on aggregate by CSKA Moscow in the second round

1993/94

First time that the European Cup champions hadn't

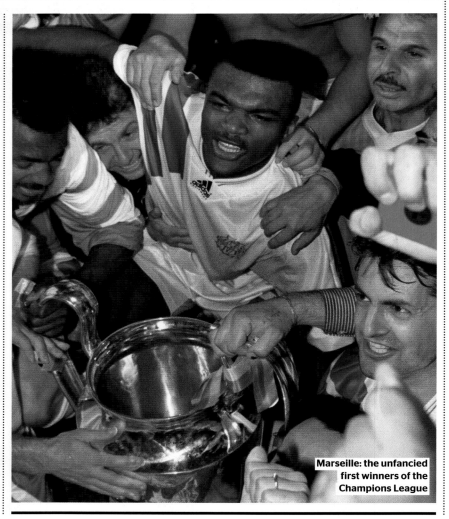

Marseille: the unfancied first winners of the Champions League

defended their title (a match-fixing scandal meant UEFA had no choice but to disqualify Marseille)

■ AC Milan won their fifth title overall, and their first Champions League title, trouncing Barcelona 4-0 in the final

■ **Marcel Desailly became the first player to win consecutive European Cups with two teams**

1994/95

■ Ajax, of Amsterdam, won the competition without losing a game, either in the group or the knock-out stages, and lifted the trophy for the first time since 1973

■ **The first year in which eight teams advanced to the knock-out stage and the first final to feature corporate sponsors on players' shirts**

1995/96

■ First tournament in which UEFA introduced three points for a win instead of two – the governing body wanted to encourage more ruthless attacking play

■ **The trophy was won by the 'Girlfriend of Italy', Juventus, who beat defending champions Ajax on penalties in the final. It was their first championship trophy since 1985 and the first final to be decided on penalties since 1991. It was the only Champions League title that Juventus won in the 1990s, despite the fact they reached the next two finals. It was also one of only two Italian wins in the final, although a Serie A club qualified for every final for seven straight years from 1992 to 1998**

■ In Dynamo Kyiv's first group game against Panathinaikos, they were accused by the Greeks of a failed attempt to bribe referee Antonio Lopez Nieto and were subsequently thrown out of the Champions League by UEFA and banned for the two years. Aalborg BK were called in to replace them in the group stage

1996/97

■ **Borussia Dortmund became the first German side to win Europe's premier club tournament since the country's reunification. They beat Juventus 3-1 (but met them again in the UEFA Cup in 1992/93 and lost 1-6)**

■ This was also the first time Borussia Dortmund had won the trophy: Paulo Sousa joining Marcel Desailly as a player who has won the competition two years in a row, with two clubs

■ **Lars Ricken scored with his first touch, after replacing Stephane Chapuisat on 70 minutes, with a delightful chip over beefy Juventus keeper Angelo Peruzzi**

1997/98

■ Real Madrid won the big one for the first time in 32 years, beating Juventus 1-0, and signalling a glorious run of three wins in five years for *Los Blancos*

■ **First season to have six groups, as opposed to four in the previous tournament, and the first to have two qualifying rounds instead of one**

■ Champions of smaller nations returned to the Champions League, while the runners-up of some domestic leagues (including England's Premier League) were entered into the competition for the first time

■ **Kosice, the champions of Slovakia, became the first team in the history of the Champions League to finish the group stage without a single point**

■ The quarter-final between Bayern Munich and Borussia Dortmund was

Real Madrid: the first Spanish winners of the Champions League

the first Champions League meeting of two teams from the same country

1998/99

■ **The Champions League was won for the first time by Manchester United, coming back from a goal down in the last two minutes of injury time to somehow defeat Bayern Munich 2-1 in the final**

■ The Red Devils also became the first English club to win Europe's principal club football tournament since 1984 and were the first English club to reach a Champions League final since the Heysel Stadium disaster

■ **It was the first time Europe's top club competition had been won by a team who would not have qualified under the old qualification rules (title holder or national league champion). Since then, Real Madrid (2000), Milan**

Lars Ricken scored with his first touch in the 1997 final

(2003 and 2007), Liverpool (2005), Barcelona (2009) and Chelsea (2012) have achieved this feat

■ UEFA ordered Real Madrid to play one match away from their usual home ground, the Bernabéu, because of crowd trouble in their previous home match against Borussia Dortmund in the first leg of the 1997/98 semi-final

1999/00

■ **This was the first time in which an additional qualifying round was introduced to generate two group stages, firstly with 32 teams – eight groups of four – who played six matches each to reduce the competition to 16 teams for the second group stage. The eight third-placed teams were transferred to the UEFA Cup third round**

■ The 1999/2000 final was hosted in the Stade de France in Paris, the city where the

2001/02
Leverkusen: the first team to reach the final without ever winning their domestic title

roots of the competition had begun, 50 years previously

■ **The Real Madrid versus Valencia final was the first time that both Champions League finalists had come from the same country, in this instance, Spain**

2000/01

■ Bayern Munich won their first European Cup since 1976, beating Valencia 5-4 on penalties and eliminating the preceding two Champions League winners, Manchester United and Real Madrid, along the way

■ **The 2001 final was a clash between the two previous season's losing finalists: Bayern Munich, who had**

lost to Manchester United in 1999, and Valencia, who had lost to Real Madrid in 2000. Valencia became the first club to lose two consecutive finals

■ Bayern Munich's Oliver Kahn became the first goalkeeper to win the Man of the Match award in the Champions League final, saving three of Valencia's penalty kicks

2001/02

■ **A Michael Ballack-inspired Bayer Leverkusen eliminated all three English teams on their way to the final, their last victim being a David Beckham-less Manchester United in the semi-final. It was their**

first time in the final of the Champions League and they were also the first team to reach the UEFA Champions League final without ever having won their national championship. It was a busy year indeed for the Factory Squad

2002/03

■ The competition was won by Milan, who beat Juventus on penalties in the European Cup's first all-Italian final

■ **Maccabi Haifa became the first Israeli club to qualify for the Champions League group stages. Basel, of Switzerland, and Genk, of Belgium, also made their first appearances in the group stage**

2003/04

■ 2003/04 was the first competition to feature a 16-team knockout round instead of a second group stage

■ **Deportivo La Coruna lost their quarter-final first leg 4-1 in Italy against the holders Milan and nobody gave them a chance in the second leg. However, the on-form Spanish side dramatically reversed the odds to become the first side to overhaul a three-goal first-leg deficit in the UEFA Champions League. They won 4-0 to seal a quite staggering 5-4 aggregate victory**

■ FC Porto's unlikely victory in the final was Portugal's first

since 1987. This was Porto's second European trophy in consecutive years, following their UEFA Cup success in 2002/03

2004/05

■ **Defending champions, FC Porto, minus José Mourinho, were eliminated by Inter Milan in the first knockout round**

■ Liverpool played Juventus for the first time since Heysel, winning 2-1 on aggregate at the quarter-final stage

■ **Chelsea's 3-2 second-leg quarter-final defeat by Bayern Munich in the quarter-final was the last European night at Munich's Olympiastadion**

2005/06

■ Despite finishing fifth in the Premier League in 2004/05, Liverpool were granted a special exemption by UEFA to try to retain their title as holders, and were placed into the first qualification round. The governing body changed the rules afterwards

■ **The newly designed trophy is presented and lifted for the first time**

2006/07

■ When Manchester United beat Roma 7-1 in the quarter-final second leg after a 1-0 reverse in the opener, it was the first time in 23 years that United had managed to get through a European knockout match after losing the first leg

2007/08

■ **First all-English final in the history of the European Cup between Chelsea and Manchester United. United won the match 6–5 on penalties, following a 1–1 draw after extra time**

■ The first season in the competition's history that four teams from the same country – England's Arsenal, Chelsea, Liverpool and Manchester United – reached the quarter-final stage. Remarkably, it was repeated by the same teams in the 2008/09 season

■ **It was also the first time in Champions League history that a nation's clubs – England's Arsenal, Chelsea, Liverpool and Manchester United – were eliminated only by each other. Arsenal were beaten by Liverpool, who were beaten by Chelsea, who were defeated by Manchester United in the final**

■ AC Milan's 0–2 defeat by Arsenal in the second leg of the first knockout round was the club's first defeat to English opposition at the San Siro

2007/08

Arsenal became the first English club to beat Milan in the San Siro

2007/08

Barcelona's Bojan Krkic was the first Champions League scorer to be born in the 1990s

■ Catalan-born Bojan Krkic became the first Champions League scorer to have been born in the 1990s after he bagged the only goal in Barcelona's 1–0 quarter-final first-leg win against Schalke 04

2008/09

■ For the first time, both UEFA Cup finalists featured in the Champions League group stage: Werder Bremen and Shakhtar Donetsk

■ Anorthosis of Cyprus and BATE Borisov of Belarus were the first teams from their respective countries to qualify for the group stage

■ Bayern Munich defeated Sporting CP 12–1 on aggregate

in the first knockout round; the biggest two-leg win in the Champions League era.

■ Manchester United's 2–0 victory over Inter Milan in the first knockout round was their 21st consecutive undefeated match, a record surpassing Ajax's 20 undefeated matches, set between 1985/86 and 1995/96. The record was eventually extended to 25 matches, ending with the 2–0 defeat to Barcelona in the final

■ Porto's second-leg 1-0 quarter-final defeat by Manchester United was the Portuguese club's first home defeat to English opposition

■ **Manchester United were the first defending**

champions to reach the semi-finals since UEFA introduced the first knockout round

■ Arsenal's 3–1 defeat by Manchester United in the semi-final second leg was the Gunners' first defeat at the Emirates Stadium in a European competition

■ **Barcelona won the final against Manchester United 2–0, with goals from Samuel Eto'o and Lionel Messi. Barcelona's victory meant they became the first Spanish team to win a league, cup and Champions League Treble.**

■ Manchester United were the first defending champions to reach the final of the competition since Juventus

in 1997, but they failed to become the first club to defend the European Cup since Milan in 1990

2009/10

■ First time a UEFA Champions League final is played on a Saturday night

■ The two clubs competing in the final – Inter Milan and Bayern Munich – had each won their domestic league and cup competitions, which meant the winner of the Champions League would become only the sixth club in Europe – and the first club from their respective countries – to achieve a continental Treble. It was José Mourinho's Inter Milan who managed it

2010/11

■ Tottenham Hotspur, made their debut in the Champions League tournament, topped their group, dumped out Milan, but eventually lost 5-0 on aggregate to Real Madrid in quarter-finals

2011/12

■ As part of a trial that started in the 2009/10 UEFA Europa League, two extra officials – one behind each goal – were used in all matches from the play-off round onwards for the first time

■ **Chelsea and Roman Abramovich celebrate their first Champions League title**

2008/09

Barcelona became the first Spanish team to win the treble in 2009

TOP 10
FINAL
STADIUMS

The best football teams on the continent refuse to strut their stuff in any old football ground

Olympiastadion
Munich, Germany (69,250)

1 Bayern Munich and TSV 1860 Munich's old home hosted the European Cup finals of 1979, 1993 and 1997.

Did you know?
On 17 May 2012, Lyon won their second successive UEFA Women's Champions League final in the Olympiastadion, 2-1 v Frankfurt.

Stadio Giuseppe Meazza
San Siro, Milan, Italy (80,018)

5 Used for the 1965 and 1970 European Cup finals, and the 2001 Champions League final, which Bayern won on penalties.

Did you know?
Giuseppe Meazza played for both Milanese clubs and was a two-time World Champion with Italy. The stadium is located in the San Siro district.

Hampden Park
Glasgow, Scotland (52,063)

6 Hosted the Champions League final of 2002, providing the stage for *that* Zinedine Zidane volley in the 45th minute.

Did you know?
Hampden Park was the biggest stadium in the world when it opened on 31 October 1903, with a capacity in excess of 100,000.

Old Trafford
Manchester, England (75,811)

7 Hosted its first major European club football final in 2003, Juventus v Milan, the only one to finish 0-0 after extra time.

Did you know?
Old Trafford is the second-largest football stadium in England, but only the eleventh largest in Europe. It was one of many designed by Archibald Leitch.

Stadio Olimpico
Rome, Italy (72,698)

2 Hosted European Cups in 1977 and 1984, Liverpool winning both, and the Champions League finals of 1996 and 2009.

Did you know?
The stadium hosted the opening and closing ceremonies of the 1960 Olympics, plus all of the athletics. In 2007, it became a UEFA Elite stadium.

Camp Nou
Barcelona, Spain (99,354)

3 Hosted the dramatic 1999 Champions League final in which Manchester United beat Bayern in the last seconds.

Did you know?
Remodelling plans, including 10,000 more seats to make it the fourth-largest sports stadium in the world, were put on hold in 2010.

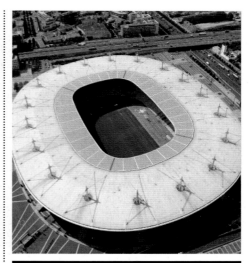

Stade de France
Paris, France (81,338)

4 The national stadium hosted the Champions League final in 2000 and 2006, Spanish teams winning both times.

Did you know?
The Stade de France was constructed for the 1998 World Cup at a cost of €290m. Michel Platini, now the UEFA president, recommended the name.

Ataturk Olympic
Istanbul, Turkey (76,092)

8 Hosted the Champions League's greatest comeback when Liverpool beat AC Milan in the final of 2005.

Did you know?
The stadium takes its name from the first president of Turkey, Mustafa Kemal Ataturk, who gained independence for the country.

Olympic Stadium
Athens, Greece (75,000)

9 Something of a good luck charm for Milan – the Italians won both finals hosted in the Olympic Stadium in 1994 and 2007.

Did you know?
The stadium's full name is Olympic Stadium Spyros Louis, incorporating the name of the first marathon winner of the modern Olympics, in 1896.

Wembley
London, England (90,000)

10 Hosted the 2011 Champions League final and will be the venue again, for the second time in three years, in 2012/13.

Did you know?
Wembley has a partially retractable roof, a 134 metre-high arch, with a span of 317 metres, and is estimated to have cost a cool £1bn.

Real Madrid
1999/00

An all-Spanish tie with an English flavour and the second of three triumphs in five years for Madrid

1 Fernando Morientes
Something of a goal machine, Morientes found his first-team opportunities with Real Madrid limited after the arrival of Ronaldo and Raúl. A successful loan period at Monaco was followed by a move to Liverpool in 2005 – which wasn't so successful. In 2006, he moved to Valencia and rediscovered some of his form, striking up a handy partnership with David Villa. Niggling injuries persisted and the rise of Juan Mata again reduced Morientes's playing time. A move to Marseille followed, but a season later, in 2010, he announced his retirement from football.

2 Ivan Helguera
The centre-back slogged on at Real Madrid until 2007, when Mahamadou Diarra's arrival reduced his playing opportunities. He headed to Valencia, but his contract was cancelled after a season and a half. Retirement followed.

3 Fernando Redondo
Having won two La Liga titles and two Champions League crowns with Real Madrid, Redondo made an unexpected move to AC Milan in 2000. However, he suffered a serious knee injury in one of his first training sessions at the club, which effectively sidelined him for two-and-a-half years. Injuries continued to plague him and he eventually called time on his career in 2004.

4 Fernando Hierro
Surprisingly prolific in front of goal, despite his defensive midfielder/centre-back role, Hierro was released by Real Madrid in 2003 after 13 highly successful years. His next challenge took him east, to Qatar and Al-Rayyan. One season later and he was ready for the glamour of Bolton Wanderers for the 2004/05 season, after which he retired.

5 Geremi
Geremi was loaned to Middlesbrough for the 2002/03 season and proved a hit, but it was Chelsea who signed him. Two Premier League titles later, he moved to Newcastle United in 2007 for three successful years, before switching to Turkish outfit Ankaragucu, then Greek side Larissa, before retiring in 2011.

6 Steve McManaman
Earning cult-hero status among Real fans and the Spanish press (the latter even saluting his androgynous likeness to Nicole Kidman), 'El Macca' left Madrid in 2003 when the arrival of David Beckham shoved him down the pecking order. He moved to Kevin Keegan's Manchester City, where things started well in the 2003/04 season. But by Christmas results were slumping, McManaman was picking up niggly injuries and his performances were suffering. The rise of Shaun Wright-Phillips meant he wasn't starting regularly and new coach Stuart Pearce released him. He retired in 2005.

TOP 5
GREAT GAMES

Five of the most rousing Champions League clashes ever

AC Milan v Liverpool
25/05/2005, final

1 Also known as The Miracle of Istanbul, this match regularly tops 'best Champions League games' charts. Liverpool, 3-0 down at half-time, looked dead and buried, but an astonishing three goals in 15 second-half minutes resulted in the game going to extra time and then penalties, which the Reds won 3-2. Bizarre.

AC Milan v Barcelona
18/05/1994, final

2 With an injury crisis developing, and key defenders Franco Baresi and Alessandro Costacurta suspended, many expected Fabio Capello's *Rossoneri* to be hammered by Johan Cruyff's 'Dream Team'. Not so. Two goals from Daniele Massaro in the first half and one each from Dejan Savicevic and Marcel Desailly in the second wrapped up one of the greatest finals.

Valencia v Lazio
05/04/2000, quarter-final (first leg)

3 An inspired Gerard Lopez led Valencia's destruction of the Serie A giants. Two minutes in and the Spanish team were already two goals to the good, with one more before half-time (in response to Simone Inzaghi's strike for Lazio) seemingly sealing the deal. Lopez completed his hat-trick after the break and Claudio Lopez scored Valencia's fifth.

Deportivo v AC Milan
07/04/2004, quarter-final (second leg)

4 Enormous underdogs against the defending champions, Deportivo had a mountain to climb if they were to make the semi-finals. Three goals later, they had wiped out Milan's first-leg advantage and were looking to go through thanks to their away goal in that same match. But a goal 15 minutes before time from captain Fran sealed their 5-4 victory in fine style.

Juventus v Man Utd
21/04/1999, semi-final (second leg)

5 Two Juventus goals in the first 11 minutes looked to have sunk United's chances of reaching their first European final in 31 years, but goals from Roy Keane and Dwight Yorke brought parity after 34 minutes. United survived a second-half onslaught from the Italian club and Andy Cole gave them victory in the 85th minute. Huzzah!